ETHNOHISTORY
of the
HIGH PLAINS

James H. Gunnerson
and
Dolores A. Gunnerson

Colorado State Office

Bureau of Land Management

Denver, Colorado

1988

DESIGNED BY: Leigh A. Wellborn

SERIES PRODUCTION: Frederic J. Athearn

FOREWORD

James and Dolores Gunnerson's ethnology of the high plains is a companion volume to the 1987 work by Dr. Gunnerson entitled *Archaeology of the High Plains*. These two documents are part of a joint USDI Bureau of Land Management (BLM) and Forest Service, USDA project to provide an overview of the archaeology and ethnology in an area encompassing eastern Colorado, western Kansas, northeastern New Mexico, and parts of Texas and Oklahoma. The original contract called for both archaeology and ethnology sections. Dr. Gunnerson developed each portion, which we are printing as separate volumes due to the massivness of the manuscript.

The ethnology of the high plains is not only interesting, but our knowledge of native relations is important to federal land management agencies that are required to consider Native American needs and concerns when making land use decisions. By knowing the ethnographic background of this region, we can be more sensitive to the desires of Indian peoples.

This volume provides both our managers and the professional community with a study that will become a standard reference for this area. I am, therefore, pleased to share this important work with you. We hope that the contribution of both the BLM and the Forest Service to the body of literature is long-lasting and useful.

State Director
Bureau of Land Management
Colorado

EDITOR'S NOTE

In editing this volume, several questions as to the distances arose. There has long been controversy over the actual measurement of a "league". the Spanish "league" was somewhat flexible in its measurement of surface distance. Modern dictionaries describe a league as a measure of about 3 miles. Pedro Vial's 18th century leagues were some 2.6 miles according to the Gunnersons. I chose to use a figure of 2.73 miles per league when converting the Gunnersons distances into modern miles. This figure is based on bibliographic references from 18th century New Mexico. As noted, a league something between 2.5 miles and 3 miles. I think that 2.73 miles represents a good compromise.

Any other conversions such as kilometers to miles are mine and represent conventional distances. Jim and Dolores Gunnerson have been most helpful in preparing this manuscript and any errors or omissions in this work are mine alone. I hope the distance conversions are helpful to the reader.

Frederic J. Athearn
Editor
Denver, Colorado
September, 1988

TABLE OF CONTENTS

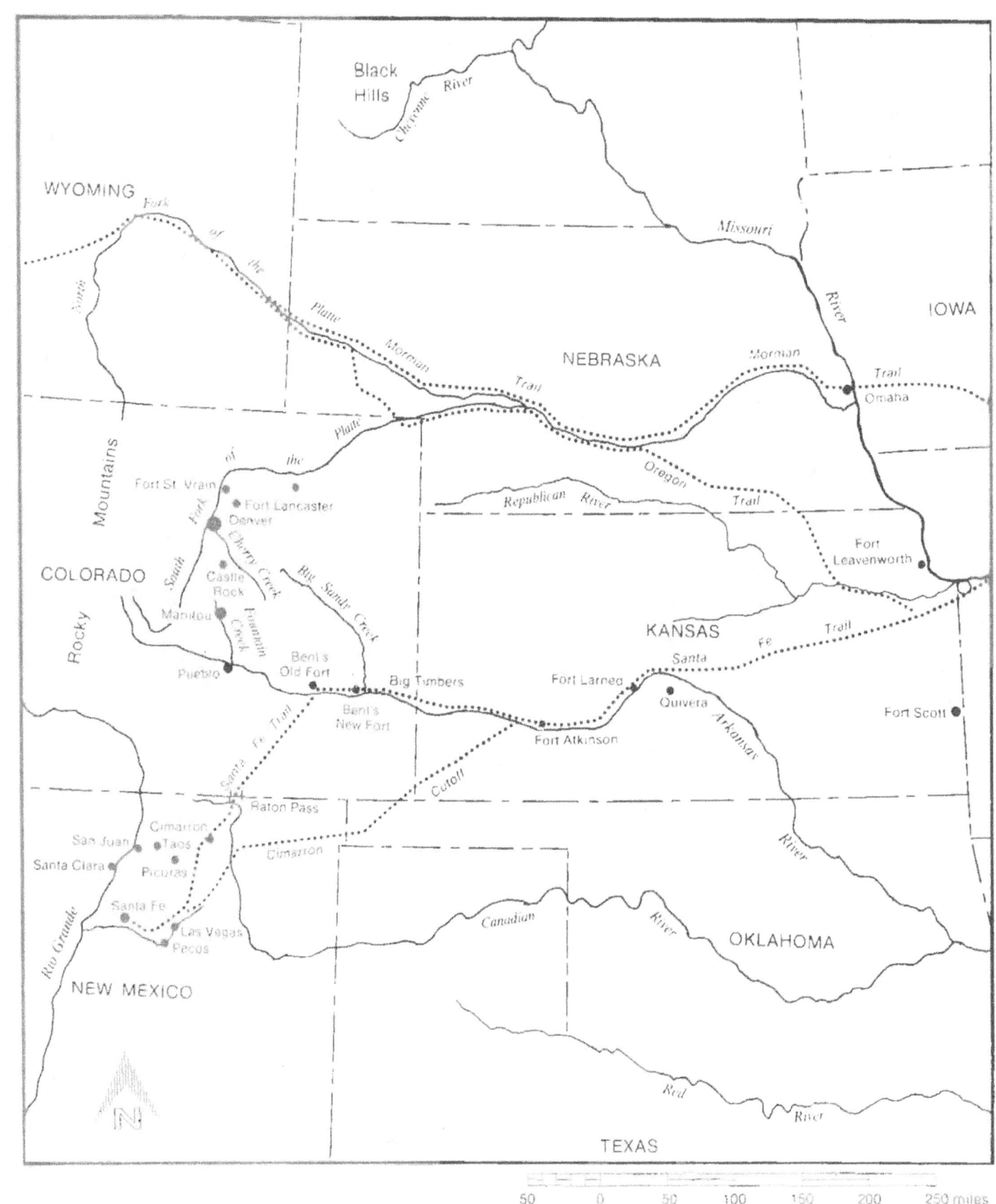

Map of the High Plains Area with Historic Locations Mentioned in this Volume

INTRODUCTION

In broad outline, native occupation of the Central High Plains can be summarized as follows. The area west of the eastern foothills of the Rocky Mountains, in south-central Colorado, was dominated throughout the historic period by Utes who joined with Comanche bands after 1706 to make forays onto the plains. The Central High Plains, *per se*, was dominated by Apaches during the 1500s and 1600s, with other tribes crossing or entering the plains only incidentally. In the early 1700s the Apaches continued to dominate the Central High Plains but Utes and Comanches moved into the southwestern corner. By the middle of the 1700s, the semisedentary Apaches were forced to abandon their villages, and for the rest of the century Comanches were the dominant force, with other tribes entering the area only occasionally. At the beginning of the 1800s, however, tribes from the north challenged the Comanches and by 1820 Arapahos, Cheyennes, Kiowas, and Kiowa Apaches had spread south to the Arkansas River, and beyond, in substantial numbers. Before and after this date Shoshonis, Blackfeet, Gros Ventres, Crow, Sioux, and Pawnee occasionally entered parts of the Central High Plains, making their presence felt by raiding Spanish installations, and/or New Mexican natives allied with the Spanish. In the mid to late 1600s, several small groups of Pueblo Indians, especially from Taos, Picuris, San Juan and Santa Clara took refuge among Apaches in western Kansas to escape Spanish retaliation after a revolt at Taos in 1640 and the larger Pueblo Revolt of 1680.

During the 1500s and 1600s, a nearly solid block of Caddoan speakers lived in permanent villages and practiced horticulture on the prairies immediately east of the Central High Plains. Various bands of Pawnee and Wichitas were the westernmost of these. Beyond, were the Siouan-speaking Ponca, Omaha, Iowa, Oto, Missouri, Kansa and Osage who especially in the 1700s, ventured west into Pawnee and Wichita hunting territory to hunt or to steal horses. When the Spaniards of Texas referred to "Nations of the North," they basically meant tribes of the Wichita confederacy in northeastern Texas and Oklahoma (Bolton 1914). When New Mexicans referred to "Nations of the North," they meant such tribes as the Kiowa, Kiowa Apache, Arapaho and Cheyenne, many of whom soon moved into eastern Colorado. During the mid-1700s the Spaniards of both New Mexico and Texas were well aware of the Comanches. They suffered badly from both the Comanche and various other hostile Apache bands. By the mid-1800s numerous tribes, including some from much farther east, were moved to reservations in eastern Kansas and Oklahoma. They, too,

occasionally ventured onto the Central High Plains to hunt, but not in significant numbers.

By the middle of the 1800s, the colorful, exuberant, horse-nomad way of life on the plains had reached its zenith and was already beginning to deteriorate. At first various tribes had their territories restricted by treaties. Later they were placed on reservations. In nearly all cases these measures resulted in armed conflict with Europeans, but the native cause was hopeless. Well before 1900, the most dramatic of "the old ways," that had flourished for only a few decades, were gone.

Alliances among the tribes of the plains often shifted; sometimes being allies, sometimes as enemies. Generally, few alliances were of long duration. Kiowa Apaches, for example, functioned as a band of the Kiowas from before 1700, probably before 1680. This was so much the case that when Kiowas are mentioned after that date, one can be reasonably sure that the Kiowa Apaches were also involved. Likewise, when Apaches are mentioned along with the Kiowas, they were the Kiowa Apaches. Just how long the Arapahos and Cheyennes were allied is not certain, but by the early 1800s the two tribes were closely associated. There were southern and northern bands of both Arapahos and Cheyennes, with the southern bands usually functioning together on the Central High Plains. The Ute and Comanche alliance, so deadly in the early 1700s, ended suddenly in 1747, when the Comanches moved east onto the plains. Soon after this break, the Jicarilla Apaches became friendly with the southeasternmost Utes and made common cause with them against the Comanches. The Pawnees were rarely involved in alliances, except with the Oto, and were generally considered enemies by other plains tribes.

Starting before 1820 and lasting until about 1860, large gatherings of Indians from most of the nomadic tribes of the Central High Plains were repeatedly noted. The involved tribes included: Comanches, Cheyennes, Arapahos, Kiowas, and Kiowa Apaches. Occasionally one or more of these tribes were not mentioned, which could reflect either their absence or incomplete reporting. Various other tribes, not listed above, were also occasionally included. These gatherings or "rendezvous" were usually at one of several specific locations. Most easterly was Fort Atkinson, sometimes called the "New Post on the Arkansas" just west of Dodge City, Kansas. It was founded in 1850 and abandoned in 1853 (Barry 1972: 965, 1170). Big Timbers, noted for its stand of cottonwood trees, was near Lamar, Colorado. Bent's Old Fort on the Arkansas, about 15 miles above the mouth of the Purgatory River, between present Las Animas and La Junta, was another regular rendezvous from the time of its founding in 1832 until William Bent destroyed it in 1849. Other large gatherings took place near the confluence of the Arkansas and Apishapa Rivers, not far from present Fowler, Colorado. These locations were all on or near the Santa Fe Trail and hence were seen or mentioned by many travelers. Also, Europeans using this trail, attracted natives, especially when the distribution of presents was expected. Farther west, rendezvous took place near Pueblo, Colorado, where the Arkansas River leaves the foothills of the Rockies and is joined by Fountain Creek. Perhaps the most important gathering place along the foothills was at the boiling springs that gave Fountain Creek its name. These are said to have been considered sacred by various Indian tribes, and the area around them was neutral ground. Hence, apparently, the modern names "Manitou" Springs and "Colorado" Springs. Called "Fontaine qui bouille" by Frenchmen and "Agua Hervienda" by New Mexicans, it seems to have been a major trading rendezvous for the latter. The Apachean name for the Arkansas River was rendered "Na-pes[h]-tle" by the Spanish and translated by linguists as "flint arrow river." It may originally have been "Na-be-esh-iel" meaning "water boiling up here and there," a term recognizing the "white water" of the Arkansas itself or possibly the springs (D. Gunnerson, personal communication). Another rendezvous point was on Cherry Creek, near present-day Denver, where the South Platte River leaves the mountains. A little farther north, about 15 miles east of Longmont, Colorado was Fort St. Vrain, also called Fort Lookout, constructed in 1837 and finally abandoned about 1851. At the northern Colorado rendezvous Shoshoni, Sioux, Blackfeet, and Crow were ordinarily present in addition to tribes frequenting the Arkansas River sites. The four westernmost locations are all essentially on the Old North Trail, followed for centuries by natives traveling along the foothills between northern Mexico (or eastern New Mexico) and the Black Hills, or Upper Missouri River areas. In the late 1800s the Goodnight-Loving cattle trail followed much of this route, as does today's Interstate Highway 25.

Rufus B. Sage (1956 II: 274-275) described an intertribal Sun Dance held in late August 1843 near Fort Lancaster (later called Fort Lupton) northeast of Denver, where nearly a thousand lodges of natives were assembled. Most were apparently Arapahos and Cheyennes, but also present in large numbers were Sioux, Comanches, Blackfeet, and Arikaras. Other authors mention large "medicine lodges" in the same general area, but their descriptions are far less detailed than that of Sage.

During most of the nineteenth century there is often mention of a few natives of one tribe living or fighting with a group made up primarily of those from one or two other tribes. Apparently the members of an entire tribe were seldom all together, usually functioning instead as several distinct bands. In some cases these bands appear to have had a political identity that was maintained for a number of years or even generations, with the bands occasionally joining together for hunts, ceremonies, or especially after about 1850, defensive military action.

CHAPTER ONE

THE APACHE TRIBES

Many tribes are known to have been on what is here called the Central High Plains, but only seven tribes occupied a significant portion of the area for any length of time. These seven, with their linguistic affiliations were: Athabascan—Apache and Kiowa Apache; Kiowan—Kiowa; Shoshonean—Ute and Comanche; and Algonquian—Arapaho and Cheyenne. The Siouan speaking Crow, Blackfeet, and Dakota frequently appeared from the north as did the Caddoan speaking Pawnee and Wichita from the east. These 12 tribes are those primarily dealt with here. Once the Apachean two-century domination of the area east of the mountains was broken in the early 1700s, they had semipermanent villages for only about a century. The tribes were completely nomadic hunters. Tribal hunting territories were poorly defined and no group had exclusive rights to specific areas. The following overview ethnohistories are arranged by linguistic families and, more or less, by the time of arrival on the Central High Plains.

Of the other tribes that lived on the Central High Plains after European contact, the history and ethno-archeology of the Apaches are best known. This reflects the fact that: (1) the Apaches dominated the major part of the Central High Plains between initial Spanish contact and 1720, (2) that in the latter part of this period some, if not most, of the Apaches in this region lived in semipermanent villages, and (3) that these Apaches had contact, either direct or in-direct, with Spanish New Mexicans who recorded enough information for an outline of Apache cultural history. Since the Kiowa Apaches were so closely affiliated with the Kiowa, they will be discussed with that tribe rather than in this section with the rest of the eastern Apaches.

The previous homeland of the Southern Athabascans was almost certainly west-central Canada where their closest linguistic relatives lived at the time of contact and where, for the most part, they are still located. Clues to the time of a split between the Northern and Southern Athabascans and the subsequent differentiation of the latter are provided by lexicostatistical data presented by Hoijer (1956; 1971). He suggests that the Southern and Northern groups split well within the past thousand years and identifies two southern Athabascan languages: Kiowa Apachean which is restricted to the Kiowa Apache, and Southwestern Apachean which includes the rest. The latter language he, in turn, divides into two groups, separating Jicarilla and Lipan from the others. He also finds that Kiowa Apachean shares with Jicarilla and Lipan some phonetic similarities

that it does not share with the other southwestern Apachean dialects. In any case, Kiowa Apache is close to other Apachean languages. In 1801 the Kiowa Apaches attempted to affiliate with the Jicarillas and Navajos because they considered themselves, and the latter tribes, to be ethnically and linguistically one people (D. Gunnerson 1974: 289). Goddard (1911: 7-8) considered the dialects of the Apacheans mutually intelligible (D. Gunnerson 1974: 152) and Hoijer (1938) was impressed by their high degree of similarity. Furthermore, one of Opler's (1938: 383) Jicarilla informants said of the Kiowa Apache, "They speak our language; the language is just about the same." These linguistic relationships are entirely compatible with ethnohistorical and archaeological reconstructions presented by Gunnerson and Gunnerson (1971) and D. Gunnerson (1974). In brief, the Gunnersons suggest that the Apacheans arrived in the Southwest as a more or less homogeneous group. The ancestors of the Jicarilla, Lipan, and Kiowa Apaches remained to the east of the others, and they maintained a plains orientation. Until the 1720s, the Apacheans were all in contact (not always friendly) with one another and had at least tenuous contacts with the Northern Athabascans (Gunnerson and Gunnerson 1971). The Kiowa Apaches, on the northern edge of Plains Apacheria, were the most remote and in the 1720s were cut off from other Apacheans by the Comanches. Having thus become a very small, isolated group, they joined the more powerful Kiowa near the Black Hills (South Dakota). Later they moved to the Southern Plains with the Kiowa, who influenced their culture heavily. By about 1730 the rest of the plains Apache bands were forced off the Central High Plains, mainly by pressure from Comanches and Utes to the west, and Pawnees to the east. But they retained contact among themselves.

Fortunately for historians, the arrival of Apacheans in the Southwest did not long precede Francisco Vasquez de Coronado's *entrada*. Pueblo groups, whose oral traditions included the event well into the 20th century, were able to tell Spaniards that the Apacheans (called "Teyas" and "Querechos" by the Pecos and Jemez people then and now) had arrived only 16 years before the Spaniards, or about 1525.

Although various lines of evidence--archeological and linguistic as well as history and oral tradition--support that date, and there is literally no evidence to the contrary, there are still a few scholars who hold a contrary opinion. Jett

(1964) and Brugge (1979, 1983) hold that Athabascans might have arrived in the Southwest as early as A.D. 1000-1300 and might have been responsible, at least in part, for the abandonment of many Pueblo sites in the 1100s and 1200s. The lack of evidence for the presence of Athabascans in the Southwest before the 1500s relegates such ideas to the realm of speculation.

A possible reason for the Apachean migration southward has been advanced by D. Gunnerson (1972; 1974), who suggested that they chose to migrate from the north at the maximal stage of the "Little Ice Age." They may have followed rapidly increasing herds of bison down the plains when, according to Bryson, Baerreis and Wendlund (1970), conditions changed for the better after severe droughts in the mid-1400s. This explanation is compatible with the dates for linguistic splitting of Northern and Southern Athabascans as obtained by lexicostatistics, and with the idea of a rapid Apachean migration south via the High Plains just east of the Rocky Mountains. Alternative routes have been considered (Huscher and Huscher 1942; Steward 1936: 62), but there is no particular evidence to support them.

Ethnohistorical evidence indicates that the Apacheans arrived in the southwest as nonceramic, bison-hunting, nomads (Hammond and Rey 1940: 261; D. Gunnerson 1956; 1974: 17-18). Such people would not have left easily identifiable archeological sites unless their nonceramic artifacts included distinctive items, and for early Apacheans this seems not to have been the case. Their sites of the 1500s may prove to be campsites with an unspecialized plains-like stone inventory and perhaps limited amounts of eastern Pueblo "trade" pottery, especially from Pecos [Pueblo]. On the plains of western Kansas and Nebraska, and eastern Colorado and Wyoming, where one might expect to find prepottery Athabascan sites, none have thus far been identified. Apachean sites in this area are all assignable to the Dismal River aspect and date from the 1600s and early 1700s (J. Gunnerson 1959, 1968; Gunnerson and Gunnerson 1971; Schlesier 1972; D. Gunnerson 1974). These sites yield not only diagnostic pottery but also a few distinctive stone tools, and some houses that deviate from plains patterns. Because of the geographical position of Dismal River sites near the most probable Apachean migration route, earlier writers found attractive the idea that the Dismal River aspect might represent the undifferentiated ancestors of all Southern Athabascans. However, this suggestion can be ruled out, since there is no evidence that the Dismal River aspect per se existed until well into the 1600s, when the plains Apacheans took up horticulture. Details of the fusion during the late 1700s, of remnants of the Dismal River Apaches with New Mexican Jicarilla Apaches have been presented by D. Gunnerson (1974: 211-214).

When Coronado crossed the High Plains in 1541, going as far north as central Kansas, he found the area covered with high grass and occupied by bison-hunting, dog-nomad Apaches (Teyas and Querechos), already specifically adapted to life on the plains. Castaneda, one of Coronado's men, learned from the Pueblo peoples (probably at Pecos) that a group called "Teyas" had first appeared in the area some 16 years before 1541 as marauders who had unsuccessfully attacked Pecos and other pueblos. When their attack failed, these people made peace throughout the land, departed for the plains, and became important traders of plains products to the Pueblos (Winship 1896: 524; Hammond and Rey 1940: 258). Coronado met both Teyas and Querechos on the plains, beyond Pecos, and described both groups as highly mobile dog-nomad bison-hunters who lived in sewn skin tents. The Querechos have long been accepted by scholars as Athabascans and D. Gunnerson (1974: 17-23), following linguistic leads provided by Hodge (Mooney 1898: 245) and Harrington (1940: 512) plus ethnohistorical evidence, has demonstrated that the Teyas were also Athabascans. Furthermore, Bandelier (1892: 116-120) collected at Santo Domingo, a legend that matched, in detail, Castaneda's account of the Teyas laying siege to Pecos and destroying various other pueblos. In the Santo Domingo (New Mexico) version, however, it was the Kirauash (Querecho), not the Teyas who were the raiders, so that both groups are specifically linked to an invasion in Pueblo lore.

In 1593 the Humana Expedition went out onto the plains, by the way of Pecos, and encountered Vaquero Apaches. The only member of the party to survive was a Mexican-Indian servant, Jusepe Gutierrez, who was captured by, and lived for a year with, the Vaquero Apaches where he learned their language. He eventually escaped to New Mexico and made contact with Juan de Onate in 1598 who recorded his account and later used him as a guide and interpreter (Hammond and Rey 1953, 1966 Passim; D. Gunnerson 1974: 54-55).

Accounts of later Spanish expeditions corroborated what Coronado and his men had said about the plains nomads, but even Onate, who led the first permanent colonists to New Mexico, added little that was new concerning the plains Apache lifeway. However, he was the first to record "Apache" as the name for both the plains hunters and the "wild tribes" who, sometime in the half century after Coronado's journey, had taken over the country between the various Pueblos. Actually, Onate applied the name first to the inter-Pueblo Athabascans who, by the time of his arrival in 1598, were stealing corn from the Pueblos. "Apache" is the Hispanicized version of the Nahuatl (including Aztec) word "mapachtle," the name for "raccoon," still used in New Mexico. In using this name for the Western Apaches, Onate was probably labeling them thus not only because of their raids on cornfields, but they probably also painted the area around their eyes black, like the raccoon's mask, as the Jicarilla did later. Actually, the Aztec glyph for the raccoon featured its "hands," and its facility at using them. In modern Mexico a derivative of "Mapachtle" is a standard term for "thief," and in the "shame culture" of the Apacheans, stealing is to be regretted only if one is caught. The extension of the name "Apache" to the plains hunters, who were careful not to offend the tribe's Pueblo and, later, Spanish trade friends, undoubtedly reflected Spanish recognition that all the Athabascan tribes surrounding New Mexico spoke the same language.

Soon after his arrival, Onate started accumulating information on the natives (Hammond and Rey 1953; D. Gunnerson 1974: 55-74). He equated the Querechos with Apaches, and distinguished between those Apaches living in the mountains near Picuris and Jemez from the Vaquero Apaches living out on the plains. Onate, presumably writing from San Gabriel, just north of Espanola, New Mexico, states of the Apaches that: "Although I was told that they live in rancherias, in recent days I have learned that they live in pueblos the same as the people here. They have a pueblo eighteen leagues [50 miles] from here with fifteen plazas" (Hammond and Rey 1953: 484). This distance could put these Apaches in the eastern foothills of the Sangre de Cristos. It is interesting to speculate that these were ancestral Jicarillas who, by then, were living in permanent villages of adobe houses and who were cultivating fields as were the Jicarilla a century later in the same general area.

In 1598 Vicente de Zaldivar, one of Onate's officers, set out to explore the buffalo plains. Eleven leagues (30 miles) beyond Pecos Pueblo, probably on the Canadian river, he began to meet Vaquero Apaches, with well made skin tents and pack dogs, who had been trading at both the Taos and Picuris Pueblos (Hammond and Rey 1953: 398-405; D. Gunnerson 1974: 61). In 1601 Onate crossed the plains to Quivera, taking Jesupe as a guide. He corroborated Coronado's observations of 60 years earlier. He reported that they occasionally found *rancherias* "inhabited by people of the Apache nation" who had no permanent settlements but who followed the "cattle" as they roamed. Onate's party had no trouble with the Apaches who in no way threatened to harm them (Hammond and Rey 1953: 749).

D. Gunnerson (1974: 68) pointed out that the Vaquero Apaches, who brought the Pueblos large quantities of bison products for trade, were friends of the Pueblos whereas those bands of Apaches who lived between the Pueblos, and competed with them for the limited game available, tended

to be enemies of most Pueblos, although each band may have maintained good relations with one pueblo or another. Between 1625 and 1629 Fray Alonso de Benevides was in charge of the Franciscan mission in New Mexico. In 1630 he wrote a *Memorial* (Ayer 1916) and in 1634 a *Revised Memorial* (Hodge, Hammond, and Rey 1945) in which he described conditions in New Mexico (D. Gunnerson 1974: 77-84). In his description of the locations of various bands of the "huge Apache nation," he stated that Quinia Apaches were both west of the Rio Grande, and near Taos. Apparently some of the Quinia Apaches also lived across the mountains, east of Taos. Zarate-Salmeron, writing in 1626, was told that a better route to the plains, and Quivera, than the one Onate had taken would be via Taos and through the "lands of the great Captain Quinia." Benevides recognized that Captain Quinia was chief of the Quinia Apaches and lived ten leagues (27 miles) from Taos (D. Gunnerson 1974: 70, 78). Since the Quinia Apaches were in a location later occupied by the Jicarilla [Apache], and the modern Mescalero [Apache] name for the Jicarilla is "kinya-inde," or Kinia people, we can be reasonably certain that the Quinia Apaches were ancestors of the Jicarilla. Benevides gave the location of the Vaquero Apaches as up and down the plains, east of the Rio Grande, and provides a description of their lifeways:

> "With these hides they trade through all the land and gain their living. And it is the general dress as well among Indians as Spaniards, who use it as well for service as bags, tents, cuirasses, shoes (*calcado*), and everything that is needed.... When these Indians go to trade and traffic, the entire rancherias go, with their wives and children, who live in tents made of these skins of buffalo (*sibola*), very thin and tanned; and the tents they carry loaded on pack-trains (*requas*) of dogs, harnessed up with their little pack-saddles, and the dogs are medium sized. And they are accustomed to take five hundred dogs in one pack-train, one in front of the other; and the people carry their merchandise (thus) loaded, which they barter for cotton cloth and for other things which they lack." (Ayer 1916: 55-56).

In the 1630s conflict between the Church and State in New Mexico became very serious and dissention soon spread to the natives who were exposed to great pressure from both Spanish factions. In 1639, or 1640, a group of Taos residents fled to the plains and took refuge among the Apaches of "El Cuartelejo." No contemporary account of the flight and return of the Taos has been found, but Elcalante, in a history of New Mexico, written in 1778

3

(over a century after the events), states that in about 1662 Juan de Archuleta led an expedition to "El Cuartelejo" to bring back the [Taos] fugitives (Twitchell 1914: 279-280). A 1665 document, much closer to the time of the flight, referred to it as having been about 1640. In 1638 or 1639, a party sent to Quivera by Governor Rosa killed many friendly Apaches and captured others to sell [as slaves] in Nueva Viscaya [Mexico]. This might have had some connection with the flight of the Taos to the plains (D. Gunnerson 1974: 88-89, 98). In 1640 plains Apaches were coming into Pecos [pueblo] to trade and to live there for extended periods, probably during the winter. The Pecos natives, in turn, used some of the items acquired from Apaches to pay tribute to the Spanish (D. Gunnerson 1974: 88-89).

Another band of Apaches, the Achos, were also in the Taos area and may have been the Quinia Apaches by a different name. An account, written about 1690, told of the Acho's making war on the Taos and Picuris, and also of threatening Pecos in 1646. Since the Achos are named in connection with the Pueblo Rebellion of 1680, when at that time they were allies of the Taos, it is possible that the author of the 1646 report projected the name Acho back, on the assumption, or with the knowledge, that the Achos and the Quinia Apaches were one and the same (Forbes 1960: 143; D. Gunnerson 1974: 91, 92).

During the 1640s and 1650s there was a substantial increase in the Spanish capture of Apaches; and either keeping them as slaves or selling them. Presumably some of the Pueblos also became involved in this slave trade (D. Gunnerson 1974: 92-96). Large parties of plains Apaches stopped coming into the Rio Grande valley to trade, but rather concentrated on their trading at Pecos or out on the plains where Spaniards sought out the Apaches. Also, during the 1650s, the Apaches brought captured Caddoan speakers, especially from Quivera, to New Mexico to sell to the Spanish.

In the 1670s, during the preludes to the Pueblo Rebellion of 1680, various bands of Apaches conspired with some of the Pueblos, but they did not play key roles in the uprising. One can assume that during the period from 1680 until 1692, while the Spanish were out of New Mexico, that there continued to be alliances between each Apache band and one or more of the Pueblos, even as animosity existed with other Pueblos. This was still the pattern during the post-reconquest years. There was an apparent attempt by the Spanish to establish good relationships with Pecos Pueblo and their friends, the Faraon Apaches, from whom much needed bison meat and hides were secured. During the 1690s, Apaches still dominated the high plains, and the natives of Quivera were apparently still their neighbors to the east, in central Kansas. In 1696 some of the Pueblos, especially from Picuris, took refuge among the Cuartelejo Apaches, on the plains, in order to escape Spanish pressure. Diego de Vargas started out to the plains to return them, but he never got out of New Mexico. In the foothills of the Sangre de Cristos, *rancherias* and recently destroyed huts, noted by Vargas as he made his first trip across the mountains, had probably been hastily abandoned by Apaches. Just to the north of the Taos area, Apaches, probably Acho, lived on the Colorado (Red) River (D. Gunnerson 1974: 100-125).

The name "Jicarilla Apaches" shows up for the first time in 1700 documents (D. Gunnerson 1974: 167). The Jicarillas were then living around Taos, and to the east, although no specific locations are given. In 1702 it was reported that "the Apaches del Acho, — de Jicarilla, — de Trementina, — de los Llanos, Faraones, and Chilimos and the Janos, Utes and Navahos were all at peace" (J. Espinosa 1942: 337 n 76).

A few documents are especially rich in ethnohistorical information regarding the plains Apaches during the period in which they were semisedentary horticulturalists. The earliest one is the diary of Juan de Ulibarri for his 1706 journey from Santa Fe to what is now west-central Kansas to bring back to New Mexico Pueblo runaways, primarily Picuris, who fled there in 1696 (Thomas 1935: 59-77). It has been possible to reconstruct Ulibarri's route in considerable detail (Gunnerson 1984). He went through the land of the Jicarilla, directly across the mountains east from Taos, and from there he took a nearly straight line northeast across the territory of the Pexayes Apaches, near the southeastern corner of what is now Colorado. Then he went on to the territory of the Cuartelejo Apaches, among whom the Picuris were living. It is fortunate that we do have this diary for it was in that year the Comanches and Utes first ventured out onto the plains to attack various Apaches. By the time of the next major *entrada*, northeast from New Mexico, that of Antonio Valverde in 1719, much of Apacheria was in disarray from repeated Comanche and Ute depredations.

Ulibarri met Conexeros, Achos, and Rio Colorados in the land of the Jicarilla, probably on Cimarroncita Creek, 3 miles south of the location of Cimarron, New Mexico. These Apaches told him of others, the Pexayes, Flechas de Palo, Lemitas, and Trementinas who he would meet farther east. When he camped at the foot of Laughlin Peak, 24 miles southeast of the location of Raton, New Mexico, still other Apaches of La Xicarilla, Flechas de Palo, and Carlana, came to meet him, apparently from the mesas east of Raton. Each band had its own leader, but the head chief was a Jicarilla leader called in Spanish "El Cojo," or "the lame one." Ulibarri was told that when he returned he would find them all, along with the followers of Chief Ucate, in the villages of the Jicarillas (on Ponil Creek, at the east edge of Cimarron, New Mexico).

As Ulibarri continued northeast he passed the Hill of La Jicarilla (Capulin Mountain) and camped near Penxayes Apache villages in the canyon of the Dry Cimarron River, about 11 miles west of the Oklahoma border. Here he left the canyon, and shortly before reaching Two Buttes [in Colorado], he overtook six Penxayes Apaches who were on their way to join with others in order to defend themselves from Utes and Comanches who were coming to attack them. The next day, between Two Buttes and the Arkansas River, he met three other Penxayes.

Ulibarri did not meet any other natives until he came to the first Cuartelejo Apache village 20 miles northwest of the location of Scott City, Kansas. The next day he moved to the principal village of the Cuartelejo Apaches, on Ladder Creek 14 miles north of Scott City. There he was met by "many chiefs of the settlements of El Cuartelejo." Ulibarri stayed here for nine days, but sent out three groups of soldiers to other Cuartelejo villages to bring in the Picuris Indians who were living there. The most remote Cuartelejo village was said to be 40 leagues (109 miles) away putting it in southern Nebraska. Ulibarri learned from the Cuartelejo Apaches that the Pawnees and Jumanos (Wichitas) were their (the Apaches) enemies, that there were Frenchmen among the Pawnees, and that the Pawnees lived in two large villages, seven days away over level ground. Since under good conditions Ulibarri traveled about 34 miles a day, this distance could put the Pawnees on the Loup River near its confluence with the Platte, their known location. The Cuartelejos, who were about to harvest their crops, lived in huts or little houses. When Ulibarri returned to the Jicarilla villages on the Ponil, he learned that: "the Utes and Comanches had attacked two *rancherias*; one of the Carlana and Sierra Blanca tribe, the other of the Penxayes tribe."

Although the Apaches northeast of Santa Fe, most of whom eventually joined together to be known as the Jicarilla, were friendly toward the Spanish, another band, the Faraone Apaches, who eventually became a major part of the Mescalero [Apache], were unfriendly. By the summer of 1715 the Faraone Apaches had stolen so many horses and committed other depredations in the New Mexican settlements that a punitive campaign, led by Juan Paez Hurtado, was planned. Various documents relating to this expedition, including Hurtado's diary, were related by Thomas (1935: 80-98). It is specifically stated that the Faraon were also called the Chipaynes or Limitas and, in their own language, Sejines. They are also distinguished from the Jicarilla from whom they stole animals. The Faraones lived on the plains east of Santa Fe and were regular visitors to Pecos Pueblo with whom they were very friendly. The Faraones were said to plant corn in late April or early May, harvest it in August, and store it underground. After harvest they left their villages to hunt until it was again time to sow. Their *rancheria*, closest to Picuris Pueblo, was said to: "be composed of thirty houses of wood entirely smeared with clay outside, which is located on the banks of a river, there are ten days marching with sufficient water every day because the springs are large." (Thomas 1935: 82).

Hurtado went out by the way of Picuris and Mora, so as to avoid Pecos because he was afraid that the Pecos would alert the Faraones. He traveled 16 days, in general following the Canadian River, probably into the Texas panhandle, and recorded traveling some 123 leagues (335 miles), but with many changes in direction. He never did make contact with the Faraones and did not mention even finding any of their *rancherias*.

In 1719 Governor Antonio Valverde, with a very substantial party, went from Santa Fe to what is now central eastern Colorado to chastise both Utes, and Comanches, who were harassing Spanish installations in New Mexico. The diary of this expedition (Thomas 1935: 110-133) was in sufficient detail that his route could be reconstructed with great precision (Figure 2 and Tables 3 and 4; Gunnerson 1984). He crossed the Sangre de Cristos east of Taos, reported Jicarilla settlements in the mouths of the canyons of Rayado and Cimarroncita Creeks and described in detail the Jicarilla settlements in the lower Ponil Canyon at the eastern edge of what is now Cimarron, New Mexico, as follows, (Thomas 1935: 115):

> "Their chief is the one whom they call El Coxo [who] on this occasion was absent because he had gone to the Navajo province. This news his two sons gave, who, as soon as they had tidings of the arrival of the governor, came out with the rest of their people to see him. He received them with his accustomed kindness, entertained, fed them and gave them tobacco. These said that on the very site and spot where the camp was placed, the Comanche and Ute enemies had attacked a *rancheria* of their nation, causing sixty deaths, carrying off sixty-four women and children, burning and destroying a little house in the shape of a tower which

was there, and even the heaps of maize. There were none of their possessions that were not destroyed. For this reason, they had deserted that locality a year ago and had gone up the river to live. Since that had happened they were sad and filled with misgivings and fear that the enemy might return and finish them entirely. Upon hearing this, the governor consoled them: with explanations and kind words, telling them that he had already set out on a campaign to punish this nation which had caused such great damage to all of them. They received this news with much exulting.

On this day, about three in the afternoon, the senor governor mounted his horse in company with the reverend father chaplain, the captain of the presidio, Don Joseph de Tagle Villegas, his lieutenant, Francisco Montes Vijil, and some soldiers and, marching up the river a distance of a league and a half, found seven terraced houses where some Apaches lodged. They welcomed the senor governor with great rejoicing. At the same time it was observed that many women and children, a mob of heathens who heard the bustle and confusion at the arrival of the governor, fled to the hills. It was seen that they had already gathered their crops of corn because they had placed it in the shape of a wall about a half a yard high. Many rows of the same [torn out] abundance, from which it was evident that the land is very fertile. On it they have many ditches and canals in order to irrigate their fields. Some had not finished harvesting and there was much corn in heaps not yet husked."

After leaving the Jicarilla on the Ponil, Valverde continued northeast, crossed Raton Pass and followed the foothills of the Rockies north to about the present site of Colorado Springs. From there he went northeast to near the location of Limon, Colorado, followed down the Big Sandy and cut south to the Arkansas River. Chief Carlana and a group of his Sierra Blanca Apaches accompanied Valverde as guides and spies in this, their former territory. Enemies were never contacted although their trails and camps were found. Valverde was met by several Cuartelejo Apaches who informed him that a large group of Cuartelejos wanted to meet him. He awaited their arrival on the Arkansas River near the mouth of the Purgatory. With the Cuartelejos were some Paloma Apaches, also called Calchufines, who had joined them after being forced from their homeland by Pawnees and Wichitas, with French support. Their homeland

was said to have been in the most remote part of Apacheria, probably in what is now western Nebraska, north of the Platte River. Much of the information that Valverde collected was from a Paloma with a gunshot wound that he had acquired as they were being driven out.

Ulibarri described the Apaches from El Cuartelejo who came to meet him on the Arkansas River as follows: "They numbered more than two hundred tents, and more than three hundred Indians under arms. Together with the crowd of women and children there were probably more than one thousand persons. As soon as they arrived and were encamped in the form according to their custom and military arrangement, they came to see the governor .... [Valverde] saw the dogs, on which were loaded the poles for tents and other utensils they used." (Thomas 1935: 131).

In June 1720 a Spanish party under Pedro de Villasur went through the lands of the Jicarilla, Carlana and Cuartelejo Apaches on the way from Santa Fe to Pawnee territory, near the confluence of the Loup and Platte River. Unfortunately we learn very little about the Apaches from this expedition since it was almost entirely wiped out by the Pawnee and their French allies. Only the last few days of the diary of the expedition survived (Thomas 1935: 133-137). The massacre of this party virtually ended Spain's hopes for dominating the area north and east of New Mexico since most of the New Mexicans knowledgeable of this area died along with Villasur. The French were now clearly in control and the Spanish apparently did not send out another party to Pawnee territory for three quarters of a century.

In 1723 Juan Domingo de Bustamante visited the valley of La Jicarilla at the request of these Apaches who were seeking Spanish protection against the Comanches (Thomas 1935: 193-219). Bustamante also found Jicarillas, led by Chief Cojo, along with lesser chiefs, along the foothills from the Rayado to Ponil Creek. Also still living here was Chief Carlana of the Sierra Blancas, at least six of his captains and 50 young men. A presidio was never built in La Jicarilla as had been recommended and soon the Jicarilla moved to near Ranchos de Taos where a mission was established for them in 1727.

Following Bustamante's 1723 accounts of plains Apache groups, information on them is very sparse for the next three decades. D. Gunnerson (1974: 211-217) had provided an excellent summary of the movement and realignment of these closely related groups during this period. In 1726 El Cuartelejo was still occupied by Cuartelejo and Paloma Apaches who had been joined by some of the Carlanas, previously more closely allied with the Jicarilla. By 1730, however, Cuartelejo, Paloma and Carlana Apaches were developing closer ties with the Jicarilla and lived with them in the Sangre de Cristos. In 1733 some of these Apaches returned to their "place of origin" more than 100 leagues (273 miles) to the north, presumably back to the area of El Cuartelejo. This was of very short duration since before 1748 all of the area east and northeast of Taos was abandoned by the Apaches. In that year Codallos reported that "in times past" there were Jicarilla Apache villages with "houses, palisade huts and other shelters" along the eastern foothills of the Sangre de Cristos, but they had been abandoned by the Apaches because of Comanche attacks. Some Apaches had moved closer to Taos Pueblo and others nearer Pecos Pueblo (Twitchell 1914 I: 148-150; D. Gunnerson 1974: 227). Although there were no permanent Apache villages in La Jicarilla by 1748, the Jicarilla continue to camp, hunt, and even sometimes plant crops there.

In 1752, there were Jicarillas and Carlanas living 15 leagues (41 miles) southeast of Pecos, while in 1752 and 1754 there were Carlanas, Cuartelejos, and Palomas living in and near Pecos Pueblo. Soon, however, the names Paloma and Cuartelejo disappear from the records, presumably subsumed under the Carlanas. Carlanas, with remnants of the Cuartelejos and Palomas, drifted south and by 1777 had made contact with the Lipans in southwest Texas. There they were known under the name Lipiyanes before they returned to northeastern New Mexico in the 1790's to become the Llanero Band of the Jicarilla (D. Gunnerson 1974: 253-255).

When, in 1760, Bishop Pedro Tamaron reached the Taos valley, probably in the vicinity of Ranchos de Taos, seven miles south of Taos Pueblo, he "encountered villages of peaceable heathen Apaches, who are gathered under the protection of the Spaniards for defense against the Comanches" (Grant 1934: 282). During the last half of the 1700s, the Jicarilla lived along the Rio Grande, essentially from the location of Espanola, north to Taos (D. Gunnerson 1974: 239-280). Starting about 1750, shortly after the Moache Utes became enemies of the Comanches, these Utes and Jicarilla became allies, a relationship that continued until the late 1800s and to some extent never did dissolve.

In 1798 and 1801, the Llanero Apaches arrived in northeastern New Mexico, insisting that they were indeed part of the Jicarilla. They functioned as one band of Jicarilla. On Humbolt's map of 1803 the "Llanero Apaches" are shown opposite Taos and Picuris, just to the east of the Rio Rojo (Canadian River) (D. Gunnerson 1974: 290-291). In a portion of Chacon's diary of 1801, he entered for May 5 [1801] a reference to "four ranchos of Gicarillas of those who lived on the plains and the rest of the Lipanes." He

soon realized the latter were "Lipiyanes or Llaneros rather than Lipanes." (D. Gunnerson 1974: 285).

In 1801, the Spanish learned that there were "Nations of the North" moving toward New Mexico. Among these nations was one that spoke the same language as the Jicarilla and considered themselves to be of the same people. These, of course, were the Kiowa Apache who had been separated from other plains Apaches for a century and who had been living with the Kiowa, another of the Nations of the North then appearing on the frontier of New Mexico. The Spanish were afraid that if these newcomers joined with their Apache kinsmen, it would create a serious threat. Such an alliance, however, did not occur (D. Gunnerson 1974: 289).

Information on the location and movement of Apaches in New Mexico during the first half of the 1800s is even more sparse. With the taking of New Mexico by the Americans in 1848, documents become more abundant. However, the Apache scene does not appear to have changed markedly from 1801. In July 1849, shortly after the United States took over New Mexico, James C. Calhoun was sent west to become Indian Agent at Santa Fe and Superintendent of Indian Affairs in New Mexico. The official correspondence of Calhoun (Abel 1915), who was also Territorial Governor of New Mexico, includes many mentions of the Apaches, in general, and of the Jicarillas in particular. Except for the Kiowa Apaches, who lived farther east on the plains, the Jicarilla are the only Apaches to occupy any part of the Central High Plains after about 1800.

In May 1851, Calhoun mentioned that Jicarillas, under Chief Chacon, were in the vicinity of San Miguel, La Cuesta (now Villanueva) and Anton Chico (Abel 1915: 350). These are all towns along the Pecos River, 25 to 35 miles southwest and south of Las Vegas, New Mexico. At the end of April 1852, some Jicarillas, still under Chacon, moved from Las Truchas to the Rio Pecos where they "intend to settle down and manufacture Tenajos (water-jars) and baskets to trade with and a number of them are beginning to plant" (Abel 1915: 529, 530). But that a talk was held with the Jicarilla at Pecos village, there is no indication as to just where on the Pecos River they were settling. It seems likely, however, that they were returning to the same general area where they were the spring before. Thus far, no reference has been found to the effect that they actually did plant along the Pecos River. As for their making pottery, Charles Bent (Abel 1915: 6), in 1846, said of the Jicarilla: "Their only attempt at manufacture is a species of potter ware, capable of tolerable resistance to fire, and much used by them and the Mexicans for culinary purposes. This, they bartered with the Mexicans for the necessities of life, but in such small quantities as scarcely to deserve the name of traffic."

In February 1850, there were Apaches (probably Jicarillas) in the vicinity of San Miguel. In a letter of February 28, 1850, Calhoun (Abel 1915: 155) states that "a party of Apaches, numbering some twenty or thirty, made a sudden descent from the high hills south of San Miguel, and on the broad road from Santa Fe to Las Vegas, killed one Mexican and wounded two others. This occurred within eight miles of San Miguel." Calhoun is in error in that the Santa Fe-Las Vegas road went east rather than south from San Miguel, but elsewhere Calhoun (e.g. Abel 1915: 186, 207) makes similar errors in direction. Eight miles, his maximum distance, from San Miguel would be approximately at Starvation Peak at the northeast corner of what, in the *Archeology of the High Plains* (Gunnerson: 1987) is called Alden's Mesa; lesser distances would be along the north base of the mesa. Thus the "high hills" from which the Apache suddenly descended most probably were Alden's Mesa on the south side of the Santa Fe Trail, especially since the terrain on the north side of the trail could not be described as high hills. There is a very high probability that these Apaches were living at the John Alden site (25SM72).

Calhoun mentions Jicarilla in the vicinity of San Miguel or Anton Chico a number of other times, but the locations are less specific. During the period 1849-1852, the Jicarilla did not live permanently in the Anton Chico area, but ranged primarily east of a line from Taos to Manzano (Abel 1915 passim). On the other hand, Calhoun does not report other tribes in the Anton Chico - San Miguel area that could have left the archaeological remains investigated there.

Calhoun, because of poor health, had to give up his position as Governor of the Territory of New Mexico and Superintendent of Indian Affairs. He was succeeded by William Carr Lane, who was inaugurated on September 13, 1852, (Abel 1941: 206-207). Starting on October 1, 1852, John Ward kept a "Journal of Daily Transactions at the Superintendency of Indian Affairs, William Carr Lane, Govr. and Supt." related in Abel (1941). Although the daily entries are very brief, they do provide clues about the Jicarilla through October 1, 1853. We learn, for example, that on December 21, 1852, Lane sent one of the Indian Agents, a Mr. Steck, from Santa Fe "to Anton Chico and from there to Las Vegas and Mora, thence to Taos and back to Santa Fe, the object of this trip is to see the Jicarilla Apaches—," and that he returned on January 19, 1853 (Abel 1941: 231, 332). This itinerary suggests that at least some Jicarillas were ranging along the foothills from Anton Chico to opposite Taos. On the other hand, Mr. Steck was

apparently stationed at Abiquiu, among Jicarillas and Utes, during most of the year of the *Journal.* The *Journal* includes several mentions of Chief Chacon, some in contexts that suggest that he and his band were settled and farming at Abiquiu. Nowhere, however, is there the suggestion that Chacon was in the Anton Chico-San Miguel area, nor are there references to permanent or semipermanent Apache settlements in that area.

In 1851, John Griener, one of four Indian Agents then in New Mexico, was to be stationed at Taos where he would be concerned with the natives of this area, including the Jicarilla (Abel 1915: 357, 393). The agency soon closed for lack of funds but was re-established there from 1853 until 1859 with Kit Carson as Agent. Jicarilla occasionally still went out onto the plains. In 1853, John W. Gunnison's party, on the Arkansas River, very near the site of Dodge City, Kansas, reported a camp of Kiowas whose warriors had joined with the Cheyenne, Arapaho, Jicarilla Apaches and a few Comanches to attack the Pawnee (Beckwith 1855: 21).

In 1854, the Jicarilla, under Chacon, fled from their villages of 77 lodges near Ojo Caliente, some 15 miles east of Abiquiu. They were pursued by U.S. Army Dragoons who destroyed the Jicarilla's possessions, all of which they had to abandon (Gardner 1963: 123). In spite of their severe losses and continued harassment, the Jicarilla attempted to cooperate with the Americans. For example, they went on an expedition against Texans with Lucien Maxwell (Goddard 1911: 250-251) and, in 1864, a group of Jicarillas and Utes went with Kit Carson to Adobe Walls in the Texas panhandle to fight a large group of Kiowas and Comanches (Goddard 1911: 250; Keleher 1964: 51-52).

The Jicarilla were still known for their pottery making in 1865 when Padre Martines, of Taos, wrote that they were "selling earthenwares to our people" (Keleher 1964: 49). There is so much of this heavily micaceous pottery at Spanish-American house ruins along the eastern foothills of the Sangre de Cristos that it is sometimes difficult to tell them from late Jicarilla sites. Probably most of the so-called Taos bean pots, widely popular in the late 1800s, were actually of Jicarilla manufacture.

Among Jicarilla texts collected in 1909 (Goddard 1911) are accounts of the movements of Jicarillas for various reasons. Although no dates are given, the internal evidence suggests that most of these moves took place in the last half of the 1800s, especially the third quarter. The place names mentioned indicate that the area traversed extended from Pagosa Springs, Colorado on the northwest, to the Arkansas River on the northeast, to Portales, New Mexico (and beyond) to the southeast, and south to Ruidoso, New Mexico. The place most referred to was Cimarron, New Mexico from where many of these journeys started. Often in these traditions, the Jicarilla were in the company of Utes.

In 1862 the U.S. Government negotiated a 25-year lease for 2000 acres immediately northeast of Cimarron, and built a school and council chamber for the Jicarilla and Moache Utes, along with a house for their agent. But in 1876 the agency was discontinued. Although the Utes and Jicarilla were generally miserable, they did not want to leave this area which they claimed was rightfully theirs. In 1874 a reservation for the Jicarilla was established north of the San Juan River in northwestern New Mexico, but the Jicarilla objected to being removed from the Abiquiu-Taos-Cimarron area. They were never moved to this new reservation. It was then proposed that the Jicarilla be put with the Mescalero Apaches on their reservation, but both tribes resisted and again the Jicarilla did not move. In 1880 a reservation was established westward to Tierra Amarilla, New Mexico and the Jicarilla were soon moved to it. In May of 1882 part of the Plains Band (Llanero Band) of the Jicarilla left the reservation and returned to the foothills near Mora, New Mexico. Here the fugitives lived better than the Jicarilla still on the reservation, and several attempts on the part of their agent to get them returned to the reservation were futile. After several moves in the Wagon Mound, New Mexico area, the Plains Band returned to their reservation in August 1882. In 1883, the Jicarilla were moved to the Mescalero Reservation. But in 1886 they left and returned to northern New Mexico. In 1887 they were permanently established near Dulce(on their 1880 reservation) with some redrawing of boundaries. This area, to the west of their homeland, was close enough that they continued to visit their old friends the Taos and Picuris. They also returned to La Jicarilla to camp and hunt (Keleher 1964: 46-65; Tiller 1983: 77-98).

CHAPTER TWO

KIOWA AND KIOWA APACHE TRIBES

The Kiowa have no close linguistic relatives, but they are remotely related to Tannoan speakers of the Pueblo Southwest. The earliest documentary data has them living in the Black Hills which matches tribal traditions (Mooney 1898: 153). Probably before 1700, the Kiowa were joined by Apachean speakers, most likely those known to New Mexicans as the Palomas. Between 1706 and 1730, the central plains Apaches were forced south and southwest by pressure from Comanches on the west, and by the Pawnee with French guns and native allies, from the east. The Kiowa Apaches, few in number, were cut off from their relatives to the south about 1719. They joined the Kiowa for protection. Although the Kiowa Apaches retained their own language, they functioned as a separate band of the Kiowas. They were usually present whenever the Kiowas are reported although they are usually not mentioned specifically. In the very early 1800s, the Kiowa, along with the Kiowa Apaches, moved south, as a tribe, into the Arkansas River area. During the 1700s individual Kiowas and Kiowa Apaches were brought into New Mexico, as were captives of other tribes. During the very late 1700s, these tribes included some from among the "Nations of the North." By the mid-1800s, the Kiowas and Kiowa Apaches roamed even farther to the southeast into Kansas, Oklahoma, and Texas. They were put on a reservation in 1868.

The Kiowa name for themselves is Ka'i gwu. The Spanish version, usually Caygua or Caigua, was very similar. Other plains tribes, including the Wichita, Caddo and Comanche, used only slightly different renditions. The Cheyenne used a slight variation of the Sioux name Wi'tapaha'tu, the Kiowa Apache called them Be'shiltcba and the Arapaho called them Ni'chihine'na (Mooney 1896: 1078). Mooney (1896: 1081) gives the name used for the Kiowa Apaches by various of their neighbors. They call themselves Na'isha or Nadi'ishade'na. They were commonly referred to by the Pawnee name Ga'taqka; Lewis and Clark called them Cataka in 1805, while La Salle called them Gatacka about 1682. In a treaty with the government, made jointly with the Kiowa in 1837, their name was given as Ka-ta-ka. The designation for them in sign language is the same as for other Apaches and the Navaho, suggesting knife whetters.

In his examination of Church Records in New Mexico for the period 1694 to 1875, Brugge (1965) noted numerous baptisms and burials of Kiowas; 1727 being the earliest entry. All were at parishes in northern New Mexico and most of the entries are from parishes along the Rio Grande,

north of Santa Fe. Most of these Kiowas, especially the earlier ones, would have been captives traded or sold into New Mexico as slaves, so these records do not necessarily indicate that the tribe was living near New Mexico. In 1733 about 100 families of Genizaro Indians, from various tribes, petitioned the New Mexican government for permission to establish their own settlement at the site of the then abandoned Sandia Pueblo. In addition to Caiguas (Kiowas) the group also included Jumanos (Wichitas), Pananas (Pawnees), Apaches, Tanos, and Utes. All had lived in various Spanish and native settlements, essentially as slaves (SANM I, No. 1208; Twitchell 1914 I: 353).

In 1753 a native woman was questioned at Santa Cruz, 20 miles north of Santa Fe, New Mexico, by Juan Joseph Lobato. She had been bought by Antonio Martin from Utes who had captured her from Comanches somewhere to the northeast. She, however, testified that she was a Kiowa who was taken, presumably from her tribe, by Comanches (Thomas 1940: 117). This is not the earliest mention of Kiowas in New Mexico but it clearly documents hostile interaction between the Comanches and the Kiowas at this time.

In the early 1790s the Kiowa still lived in the Black Hills region. They were also middlemen carrying English guns between the Mandan, who were getting them from British traders, and the Spanish of New Mexico (Nasatir 1952: I: 82). In 1804 Lewis and Clark found the English still using the Kiowas as traders (Loomis and Nasatir 1967: 91). Lewis and Clark, in 1804, (1905 VI: 100-101) located the "Cay-au-wa" (Kiowa) as roving from the Loup River and the Padouca branch of the Platte River to southwest of the Black Hills. They indicated that no traders visited the Kiowa and that they acquired only a few trinkets from other tribes.

In the *Statistical View of the Indians*, prepared from Lewis and Clark's information (Jefferson, 1806: 36-37), it is obvious that the Wetepahatoes lived with the Kiowa and were, therefore, probably Kiowa Apaches. For the number of tents, warriors and souls given for the Wetepahatoes, the comment is made in each case "including the Kiawas" and in the tabulation for the Kiawas one is referred back to the entries for the Wetepahatoes. For location, the Wetepahatoes are said to live "on the Padouca fork of the river Platte" and for the Kiowas, "on the Padouca, frequently with the Wetepahatoes." Unfortunately, the linguistic affiliations of neither is given, so it is possible that these were two separate bands of Kiowas.

The Kiowa Apaches were probably included in the tribes called Padoucas and Padoo by Lewis and Clark (1905 VI: 108) in 1804. Their location is given as the heads of the Platte and Arkansas Rivers and it is noted that the north fork of the Platte was called the Padouca Fork (the name however was sometimes applied by others to the South Fork of the Platte). Lewis and Clark stated that: "The most probable conjecture is, that being still further reduced, they [Padoucas] have divided into small wandering bands, which assumed the names of the subdivisions of the Padoucas nation, and are known to us at present under the appellation of Weteoagaties, *Kiowas* [italics mine], Kanenavish, Katteka [Gataka], Dotame, who still inhabit the country to which the Padoucas are said to have removed." They also noted that some Padoucas traded with New Mexico. This all fits well with what else is known of the Kiowa Apaches during this general period. Also, Lewis and Clark (1905 VI: 100-101) discussed the Wetapatos and the Cay-au-wa (Kiowas), both together and as separate tribes, and stated that what applied to the Ca-ne-na-vich and Sta-e-tan also applied to the We-ta-pa-ha-to and Kiowas (Arapaho and Cheyenne versus Kiowa Apaches and Kiowas). Mooney (1896: 1023) points out that Staitan is another rendition of Histaitan, the Cheyenne name for themselves. The case for the Paducas being the Kiowa Apache is strengthened by [Jacob] Fowler (Coues 1970: 55) mentioning the "Kiowa Padduce" along with the Kiowas, Arapahos, Ietans, Cheans and Snakes, whom he met on the upper Arkansas River in 1821. The Weteoagaties may also have been Kiowa Apaches but a different subband

On a 1806 map compiled from information acquired by Lewis and Clark (Tucker 1942, Plate XXXI), one finds on the headwaters of the Cheyenne River east of the Black Hills, the "Cataka tribe of Pado" and immediately north of them the "Dotame Tribe" and again to the north, the "Nimousin Tribe." Lewis and Clark (1905 VI: 102) identify the Dotame as speaking the language of the Padoucas, but do not give the linguistic affiliation of the Nemousin Tribe. They, too, could possibly be Padouca, that is Apachean, speakers, since in the remarks section is stated "Included in Cataka." This same map shows the "Wetapahato & Kiowas tribes" on the north fork of the Platte River, between the Black Hills and the Rocky Mountains.

On the 1814 Lewis and Clark map (Wheat 1954 II: Map 316) the Cataka are shown in the Rocky Mountains [?] at the head of the Quicourre (Niobrara) River and the Dotame at the head of the north branch of the Cheyenne River west of the Black Hills. These appear to be the only

Apachean speakers shown on the map. The Lewis and Clark map "Copied by Samuel Lewis from the Original Drawing of Wm Clark" published in Allen (1814 I), (Wheat 1958 II: Map 316) does not show the two forks of the Platte and places the "Wetapahato and Kiawa Tribe (sic)" on both sides of the Platte, well east of the Rocky Mountains, and extending south more than half way to the Arkansas River. No other tribes are shown in this general area. Lower down on the Platte, but still well above the Pawnee, the Kanenavish [Arapaho] tribe is shown, also on both sides of the Platte.

During 1800 Regis Loisel petitioned to build a fortified trading establishment on the Missouri River, near Pierre, South Dakota. In 1802 he built a fort on Cedar Island. He personally knew and described the Missouri as far up as the mouth of the Yellowstone which he said rose in the mountains of Nuevo Mexico. He also listed the tribes that lived on the major rivers and their tributaries. He included, among the wandering tribes, the Chayennes (Cheyennes), Caninambiches (Arapahos), Cayuguhas (Kiowas) and Catakas (Kiowa Apaches). These tribes he seems to have known first-hand since he proceeds to list others he knew only by name, including the Pieds Negros (Blackfeet) (Abel 1939: 223-239).

The presence of Kiowas and Kiowa Apaches near the Missouri River, in central South Dakota, in 1803, is entirely compatible with the habits of these natives, who first came into northern New Mexico in the 1790s, and after that moved back and forth between New Mexico and the Upper Missouri. They served largely as middlemen between New Mexicans and the Mandan and Arikara, who, in turn, were supplied by the English with superior trade goods than those available to either the French or the Spanish. The Spaniards, at first, were apprehensive about the Kiowas, and especially the Kiowa Apaches, because these Apacheans had sought to ally themselves with the Jicarilla Apaches and Navajos. The Spaniards feared such an alliance, but were soon making a considerable effort to establish trade relations with these tribes because they had English guns. In the records, the Spanish chiefly mentioned the powerful Kiowas, as did Anglo-Americans, while ignoring the smaller group of Apaches allied with them.

A band of natives, probably Kiowas, were known to the New Mexicans as Cuampes. New Mexican church records show that seven Cuampes, undoubtedly captives, were baptized in the 1730s-1760s (Brugge 1968: 30). Twenty-two Kiowas were baptized in that same period. The Cuampes are mentioned repeatedly in Spanish documents during the first quarter of the 1800s. The name appears in 1805 when they came to New Mexico to seek peace for themselves and for their allies, the "Sayenas" and the 'Aas." It was suggested that the Cuampes might have been the Arapahos, but recently D. Gunnerson (1983) has advanced convincing arguments that the Cuampes were a band of the Kiowas and that the Aas were Crows. The Aas had previously been tentatively identified as Skidi Pawnee by Simmons (1973). The Sayenas were probably Cheyennes.

In July 1805, Joaquin del Real Alencaster, Governor of New Mexico, interviewed two Frenchmen and an American (Lacroix, Terien, and Purcell) who had recently been brought into Santa Fe. These three Europeans, all from Loisel's trading establishment on the Missouri, were accompanied to Santa Fe by two Cuampe chiefs. Alencaster recorded that they [the Europeans] had been attacked by Kiowas while trapping on the headwaters of the Platte River and had taken refuge with the Cuampes. This was probably the South Platte since a Cuampe chief who accompanied the party said of the Cuampes that "a short time ago they had an establishment in the vicinity of one branch of the Platte River, about 40 leagues from the Arkansas and a little less from Taos" (Loomis and Nasatir 1967: 423-424).

We learn more about the Kiowa and Cuampes from the account given to Lt. Zebulon M. Pike by the American fur trader James Pursley (Purcell): "On....arrival at the point of destination [Fort Aux Cedres near the Mandans] his employer [Regis Loisel] dispatched Pursley on a hunting and trading tour, with some bands of the Padducas [Padoucas] and Kyaways [Kiowas] with a small quantity of merchandise. In the ensuing spring they were driven from the plains by the Sioux into the mountains which give birth to the La Platte, Arkansas, &c. &c. and it was their [Kiowa and Padouca] sign which we [Pike] saw in such amazing abundance on the headwaters of La Platte ([December 16, 1806]). Their party [Kiowas and Padoucas] consisted of near 2,000 souls, with 10,000 beasts. The Indians [Kiowas and Padoucas], went into Santa Fe, to know of the Spaniards if they would receive them friendly and enter into a trade with them. This being acceded to by Governor Allencaster, the Indian deputies returned for their bands....[Pursley] arrived in Santa Fe in June 1805" (Jackson 1966 II: 60-61).

Some authors who have discussed Purcell's "saga" have misinterpreted the chronology, believing that it was in the spring of 1804 that he met Regis Loisel and went with him up the Missouri. Loisel did not go up the Missouri in 1804. He came down river that spring, meeting Lewis and Clark on their way upriver on May 25, 1804. He died in or after August 1804. It was June 1803 that Purcell met Loisel going up the Missouri and joined him. It was that same season, as soon as they reached Loisel's post,

that Purcell (and two French companions) were sent out with some Kiowas and Padoucas to hunt and trade. The party spent two winters, that of 1803-1804 and that of 1804-1805, with the tribes before they reached Taos, accompanied by some of them, in June of 1805.

Thus, Purcell's saga is recorded, in part, in Spanish documents and was also told by him to Zebulon Pike as that officer was held prisoner in Santa Fe (Loomis and Nasatir 1967: 423-426, 455; Coues 1895: 756-758; Cox 1906: 116-117; Hafen 1971: 277-285; and Jackson 1966: 60-62). It is interesting that Alencaster recorded that it was "Cuampes chiefs" who accompanied Purcell and the two Frenchmen into Santa Fe and that in the account that Pike got from "Pursley," it was two members of the Kiowa and Padouca (Kiowa Apache) group who accompanied the three Europeans to Santa Fe.

The Cuampes continue to be mentioned in New Mexico's Spanish Archives and in Mexico City until at least 1830. For example, 120 Cuampes warriors appeared in Taos in July 1805 (Loomis and Nasatir 1967: 455). In May 1807, interpreter Juan Lucero learned from some Cuampes, on their way to the headwaters of Fountain Creek, where they expected the Spanish to come and trade with them, that they had not traded with the Anglo-Americans but they had obtained arms and munitions from other tribes (Loomis and Nasatir 1967: 452-453). In 1818, Hernandez testified that he was robbed by Cuampes and Cayguas [Kiowas], apparently on the Huerfano River, in southeastern Colorado (Thomas 1929: 149).

In 1805, the Kiowas were close enough to New Mexico to be considered (and rejected) as the group with whom Pedro Vial had a skirmish on the Arkansas River. An examination of Vial's diary places this encounter just below the mouth of the Purgatoire River, a few miles east of Las Animas, Colorado (Gunnerson 1984; Loomis and Nasatir 1967: 433-439). During 1805 and 1806 there are numerous references to Kiowas in Santa Fe's archives with clear implications that they [the Kiowas] were not far away to the northeast, most probably in southeastern Colorado (Loomis and Nasatir 1967: 440-451). Lucero's march of eleven days from Santa Fe to "the villages of the Kiowa" would fit well with this.

Weber (1971: 38), citing unpublished archives, states that: "In July 1806, Spanish carbinero [agent-interpreter] Juan Lucero arrived at some Kiowa rancherias, perhaps on the Arkansas, where he found six Frenchmen and one American." Pike, however, did not mention encountering Kiowas when he crossed southeastern Colorado in 1806, but stated that they wander on the sources of the La Platte

[Platte River] in one place and reside in the mountains of North Mexico in another (Pike 1966: 36, 52). Apparently by North Mexico he means northern New Mexico, which he defines as lying between 30° 30' and 44° North latitude. Since 44° is nearly to the northern border of Wyoming, the headwaters of both the North and South Platte Rivers would be within his "New Mexico." Pike also stated that the Kiowa were at war with the Comanches, Sioux, and Pawnee. The Kiowa were apparently reasonably close to Santa Fe in 1804 since in July, a group of Comanches came to Santa Fe "to make a campaign against the Kiowas and the Aas, in which they had been employed for 96 days without being able to meet their enemies" (Loomis and Nasatir 1967: 420).

In 1818, Cayguas (Kiowas) were located on the headwaters of the Arkansas River in southeastern Colorado (Thomas 1927: 149-152). At that time, under Chief La Estrella, they apparently were allied with the Cuampes at La Agua Geribidora (Manitou Springs at the head of Fountain Creek). This place, where many tribes, Spaniards, and Americans commonly gathered for trading rendezvous, was said to be in the land of the Cayguas (Kiowas). Reference is also made to Cayguas setting off from the Huerfano River with some Americans to look for buffalo. The Americans gave the Kiowas presents of guns and powder which the Kiowas, in turn, gave to their allies. It was the Kiowas' access to guns that had led the Spanish to cultivate this tribe in the early 1800s.

In 1820, Stephen H. Long's party (James 1822, 1823 II) traveled up the South Platte River and then southward along the foothills of Colorado to the Boiling [Manitou] Springs just west of Colorado Springs. They then went down Boiling Springs [Fountain] Creek to the Arkansas River, which they followed to the plains. In the Fowler-Rocky Ford vicinity of Colorado, they met some Kaskaias or Bad Heart [Kiowa Apache] natives on their way to the mountains. From these they learned that "the greater part of six nations of Indians were encamped about thirteen days journey below us, on the Arkansas. These were the Kaskaias [Kiowa Apaches], Shiennes [Cheyennes], Arrapahoes, Kiawas, the Bald-heads [?], and a few Shoshones, or Snakes. These nations, the Kaskaia informed us, had been for some time embodied, and had been engaged on a warlike expedition against the Spaniards on [the] Red River, where a battle was fought, in which the Spaniards were defeated with considerable loss."

"We now understood the reason of a fact which had appeared a little remarkable; namely, that we should have traversed so great an extent of Indian country, as we have done since leaving the Pawnees [in eastern Nebraska], without meeting a single savage. The bands above enumerated, are supposed to comprise nearly the whole erratic population of the country about the sources of the Platte and Arkansa, and they had all been absent from their usual haunts" (James 1823 II: 60-61). On July 27 (six days later), a portion of the Long Expedition under Captain Bell encountered numerous individuals of these various tribes near the present location of Lamar, Colorado (James 1823 II: 175).

Major Long also met a party of Kaskaias or Bad Hearts [Kiowa Apaches] on the Canadian River about 168 miles east of Santa Fe. They had been hunting near the "sources of the Rio Brassis and the Rio Colorado of Texas, and were now on their way to meet Spanish traders, at a point near the sources of the river [Canadian] we were descending" (James 1823 II: 103). Very few trade goods of European origin were noted in the possession of these natives. It was learned that this band of Kiowa Apaches frequented the country around the source of the Platte, Arkansas, and Rio Del Norte [Rio Grande] (James 1823 II: 111-112).

The portion of Long's 1820 party that, under Bell, traveled down the Arkansas River in southeastern Colorado, met Kiowas who were then allied with Kaskaya or Bad Hearts [Kiowa Apache], Cheyennes and Arapahos. Bears-tooth, an Arapaho chief, was the generally recognized leader of these diverse bands (Bell 1957: ff 191 ; James 1823 II: 176 ff). The Long party, in 1820, was somewhat puzzled by not finding any Padoucas. Bell (1957: 201) who met Cheyennes, Kiowas, and Kaskayas [Kiowa Apaches] on the Arkansas River in southeastern Colorado speculated that the latter three: "may possibly have descended from the once powerful nation of the Padoucas, if so, why not speak the same language, the interpreters say they all speak a different language—their general appearance is different, as also their disposition." He was partly correct, of course, in that the Kaskayas (Kiowa Apaches) were indeed part of the nation known as Padoucas.

In 1821 the Fowler-Glenn party encountered a large group of Kiowas near the mouth of the Apishapa River. The group included women and children, and upward of two hundred "houses." They were soon joined by a large group of Highatans (Comanches), followed by Arapahos, Kiowa Padduca (Kiowa Apaches), "Cheans" (Cheyennes) and "Snakes" (Shoshonies) until the gathering consisted of some 400 "lodges." They were also joined by six souls from Taos. Apparently the Fowler-Glenn party had happened on a pre-arranged rendezvous. Within eight days of first contact, the number of lodges had increased to 700, with an estimated 12 to 20 persons per lodge. According to Fowler, the combined camp consumed about 100 buffalos a day (Coues 1970: 55-63).

14

While traveling west on the Santa Fe Trail, Alonzo Whetmore (1832: 38) recorded in his diary for July 19 and 20, 1828, a meeting with a small party of Kiowas. At the time they were between Rabbit Ears and Round Mound, two New Mexico landmarks on the Santa Fe Trail, in the northeast corner. The Kiowas were returning from an unsuccessful horse-stealing raid against the "Chians" (Cheyennes). Henry Dodge (1836: 25) commented that a band of Kiowas, called the Upper Band, numbering 1800 to 2000 persons, and another called "Appaches of the Plains" (Kiowa Apaches), consisting of about 1200 individuals, frequented the Arkansas and Platte near the mountains to hunt buffalo, and also the area around Bent's Fort, on the Arkansas River near Las Animas, Colorado. These areas, he said, were also used by Cheyennes, Arapahos, and Blackfeet.

In 1836 Paul Legueste Chouteau, after a tour of the southwest in 1835-1836 for Montfort Stokes and General Mathew Arbuckle, reported that the Kaywahs [Kiowas]: "Occupy at pleasure during the different seasons of the year, such Parts of Comanche Country as suit their immediate convenience. This is done by full consent of the Comanches, who consider the Kaywas their closest allies. Number of Warriors (at least) 1,500. Cah-tah-kahs or a band of Apaches: Reside generally with and under the protection of the Kaywahs, Military force estimated at about 300." Comanche territory was said to extend from the Arkansas River south to the Mexican settlements and from the Rocky Mountains eastward to the Cross Timbers (Barry 1972: 305; Foreman 1933: 148). It is of special interest that the Kiowa Apaches are being called by their older name of Ka-ta-ka. Toward the middle of the 1800s, the Kiowa and Kiowa Apaches tended to roam more and more south of the Arkansas and less to the north of it. This southern area they shared primarily with the Comanches, while the area north of the Arkansas and south of the Platte was controlled, in the mid-1800s, by Cheyennes and Arapahos.

In 1843 Rufus B. Sage (1956: II: 252) reported that the area south of the Arkansas River on into the Texas panhandle, "was swarming with Cuamanche and Kuyawa Indians." In 1845 Lieutenants Abert and Peck, who traveled down the Canadian River in the Texas Panhandle, met a party of Kiowa essentially straight north of Amarillo, Texas on the Canadian River. The Kiowa were accompanied by several Crow Indians. "On inquiring the origin of their nation [Kiowa], and the cause of their having such influence, they replied that many years ago, so long as to be lost in the memory of their oldest tradition, their fathers had left a land far to the north, and coming higher, and finding the Camanches, had smoked the pipe of peace, and had remained in close friendship ever since" (Abert 1846: 42). The Abert party retained a much higher regard for the Kiowas than for the Comanches, whom they had met a day or two before. After leaving the Canadian River, Abert encountered another band of Kiowas near the future site of Pampa, Texas, close to the head of the North Fork of the Red River. From here, until the party was well into eastern Oklahoma, no more Indians were encountered although a few old camps were noted. In eastern Oklahoma they came to Creek and Quapaw villages (Abert 1846: 69). The map included at the end of this volume shows the territory of the "Comanchee and Kiowa Indians" extending across the panhandle of Texas, along the Canadian River.

Charles Bent, writing from Santa Fe in 1846, stated "that the Kayuguas [Kiowas] range through the country east of the mountains of New Mexico, subsist entirely by the chase, and number about 400 lodges or 2000 souls" (Abel 1915: 7). Butler and Lewis (1846: 13) were primarily concerned with the Comanches, but they did report that the Kioways, who numbered about 4000 and were friendly toward the United states, living "high upon the Canadian River, between that and the Arkansas, extending their rambles to the Rio Grande toward Mexico."

Thomas Fitzpatrick reported that during the spring and summer of 1848, Comanches and Kiowas were marauding along the Santa Fe Trail, but by September they reportedly had moved south. Fitzpatrick (1848: 245) wrote from Bent's Fort, where he got the information from Cheyennes and Arapahos, although earlier in the summer he had observed attacks of unnamed tribes near the site of Larned, Kansas.

In 1849 James Calhoun, on his way to Santa Fe to become Governor and Superintendent of Indian Affairs for New Mexico, met several thousand Indians; Arapahos, Cheyennes, Keoways [sic], Comanches, Utahs, and others - at the Arkansas River crossing, near the location of Garden City, Kansas. They were waiting for the return of Fitzpatrick from whom they expected to receive presents (Abel 1915: 18). Later in the same year, Calhoun reported that Apaches, Comanches, Kioways [sic], and Navajoes were committing depredations and "are known in every section of the territory" (Abel 1915: 32). In 1851 a large party of Kiowas and Arapahos attacked a Eutaw (Ute) village near the Red River some 31 miles (north) from Taos, and another village on the west side of the Rio Grande 19 miles from Taos (Abel 1915: 438).

On Parke's 1851 map (Abel 1915, Map 3) the Kiowas are shown on the north side of the Arkansas River, near the current location of Garden City, Kansas, with the Cheyennes on the north side of the Arkansas, near the Colorado-Kansas line, and the Arapahoes between them and the Rockies. The Utahs [Utes] are shown in the southeastern part of the San Luis Valley and the Jicarilla Apaches along the eastern side of the Sangre de Cristo Mountains (and the Pecos River) from Cimarron, New Mexico south to Fort Sumner. Marcy's 1852(?) map (Abel 1915, Map 4) has the designation "Kioways North and Middle Comanches" extending from the northwest corner of the Texas panhandle to approximately the center of Texas. In 1850 George A. McCall (1851: 13), in his review of the "Indians of New Mexico," states that the "Kayugas (Kiowas) occupy the area west of the Brasos, are seldom seen on the borders of New Mexico, and their population does not exceed two thousand souls."

In 1853, a camp of Kiowas was noted a mile west of, and across the Arkansas River, from Fort Atkinson, near the present Dodge City, Kansas. The camp was composed of old men, women, and children. The warriors had joined with Arapahos, Cheyennes, Jicarilla, and a few Comanches to attack the Pawnee. A very few miles down the Arkansas was a large camp of Comanches. These camps were near the eastern edge of Comanche and Kiowa hunting territory, beyond which, to the east, was the hunting territory of the Osage, Kansa, and Soks (Beckwith 1855: 21). The area around Bent's [Old] Fort, near Las Animas, Colorado, was considered to be in the heart of Kiowa, Cheyenne, Arapaho and Comanche country (Beckwith 1855: 26).

The Kiowas did not completely give up roaming in the northern part of the Central High Plains. In 1856 Francis Bryan (1857: 475), who traveled along the Republican River in southwestern Nebraska, commented that the river bottom was a favorite hunting ground for Cheyennes, Comanches, and Kiowas. A few miles farther west he noted that the area around the mouth of Frenchman Creek was the very home of the Cheyennes (Bryan 1857: 473). He apparently did not meet either Comanches or Kiowas here and it is not obvious as to where he secured the information.

CHAPTER THREE

KANSAS TRIBES, THE WICHITA

During their known history the Wichita did not have permanent villages on the Central High Plains, but they apparently did have archaeological roots in the area. As discussed in the *Archaeology of the High Plains* (Gunnerson, 1987), the Wichita may have developed through the Custer and Washita River Phases into the Great Bend Aspect, an archeological complex identified with the historic and protohistoric Wichita. The Wichita are Caddoan speakers and are thought by a linguist (Parks 1979) to have split from the Pawnee some 1200 to 1500 years ago, although glottochronology would place the split at 1900 years ago. Either would be compatible with the archeological data, although the earlier date would probably fit better.

Reconstructing the history of the Wichita is complicated by the number of names by which they have been known. As generally used, the name Wichita is applied to a loose confederacy of several tribes, or bands, who spoke essentially one language, but who lived in separate villages. Early Spanish usage apparently lumped all the people of Quivira as Jumanos, a name meaning "painted" or "tatooed," based on their practice of extensive tatooing. The Spanish called a few other tatooed groups who were not Caddoan speakers Jumanos too. In early French documents, they were generally called Paneassa, Panis, Panis piques or Panis noirs. The last two of these names, that is, "pricked" or "black" Pawnees, reflect the tatooing, and recognize their [Wichita] relationship to the Pawnees.

As the French and Spanish of Louisiana had increasing contact with the Wichitas during the 1700s, there were more and more references to the individual bands or villages under separate names. These, in turn, are rendered in an incredible array of spellings, some barely recognizable as phonetic versions of a single native word. Gradually the name of one band, now called the Wichita, came to be applied to the entire confederacy even though this band was neither the largest nor the best known. Other names among those most frequently mentioned are: Tawakoni, Waco, Tawehash, Yscani, Akwits, Akwesh, Kirikiris, Isis, Mentos, Touacara, Adeco, Ascani, Honecho, Tokane, and Itaz. Some of these were probably temporary group names. The Kichai or Kitsei lived among the Wichita, but were linguistically a little closer to the Pawnee (Swanton 1953: 306; Parks 1979; M. Wedel 1981). Also, in the late 1700s the Skidi Pawnee lived near the Wichita. Here the Wichita, when used unmodified, refers to the entire confederation while Wichita proper refers to the specific band.

Three recent publications are especially useful sources for Wichita ethnohistory. As documentation for Indian Land Claims, Newcomb and Field (in: Bell, Jelks, and Newcomb 1974: 271-341) present chronological surveys using both written documents and maps referring to the Wichita, plus the results of excavation at an important Wichita village along with a summary of Wichita culture. Mildred Wedel (1979; 1981) presents some excellent detail on Wichita ethnohistory, especially for the period prior to 1800, based, in part, on her earlier publications and on those of Waldo Wedel.

The Wichita bordered the Central High Plains on the southern two-thirds of its eastern border, but just barely extended into the area, except for hunting trips and trading activities. The Wichita, along with the Pawnee and Arikara (to the north) and the Caddo to the southeast, formed a nearly continuous block of Caddoan-speaking peoples prior to the 1700s. Although few Wichitas lived in the Central High Plains, they descended from people who did. The Wichita are among the earliest plains tribes to have been both visited and described by Europeans. In the narratives of the Coronado expedition onto the plains in 1541 (Winship 1896; Hammond and Rey 1940), the Wichita, then called the people of Quivira, were described in considerable detail. Waldo Wedel, in his extensive publications on the subject, has confirmed the location of Quivera as central and southcentral Kansas and he has identified the people there as Wichita (Wedel 1941, 1942, 1959, 1967). He also published extensively on his excavations of protohistoric Wichita (Great Bend Aspect) sites in Kansas. In 1601 Juan de Onate, colonizer and first governor of New Mexico, made a trip to Quivera where he found the Wichita living as they had in Coronado's time and presumably in the same area (Hammond and Rey 1954). Various accounts of the Coronado and Onate expeditions of 1541 and 1601 respectively, complement and support one another in their descriptions of the people of Quivira (Winship 1896; Hammond and Rey 1940, 1953). In central Kansas, along the Arkansas River, and lower parts of its tributaries, the Wichita lived in small settlements of round, grass-covered houses, dispersed among fields where they raised corn, beans, and squash. Ramadas or sunshades without walls were also present. Buffalo and deer were hunted but no fowls were kept. Clothing was made of hide rather than of cloth. Pottery was created and metates were used. There are indications that tattooing was practiced, which led to the Wichita's (among others) being called Jumanos by the Spanish and Pani Pique by the French. Archaeological evidence from sites of the Great Bend Aspect is compatible with the ethnohistorical accounts that reveal the presence of the Wichita in central Kansas for another century, although written accounts after those of Onate are quite meager.

Fray Alonzo de Benevides' *Memorial* (Ayer 1916) suggests that the Wichita were still living in central Kansas in 1630. Also, Archeleta, according to Escalante, (Thomas 1935) observed that in the 1660s the Quivera lived between El Cuartelejo and the Pawnee, putting them in central Kansas. For well over a century after Onate visited the Wichita [Quivira] in 1601, but information on this group is very sparse. Occasionally there are references, in Spanish documents, of Quivira captives being brought in by Apaches. Mildred Wedel (1981) found that maps, primarily French, showed Paniasa (Wichita) in the general vicinity of the Arkansas River, but this information was obtained secondhand by French explorers from tribes that lived much nearer the Mississippi River. There is no doubt that Wichitas still resided between the great bend of the Arkansas and the Smoky Hill River until at least 1700, as attested to by datable southwestern Pueblo potsherds recovered from Great Bend Aspect (protohistoric Wichita) archeological sites (W. Wedel 1982: 146-152). In the early 1700s, the Wichita apparently abandoned central Kansas and moved south to the Kansas/Oklahoma border. The Deer Creek site, in Kay County, northcentral Oklahoma, where an abundance of European trade material has been collected, was identified as a Wichita village of the early to mid-1700s (Bell and Bastian 1967; Sudbury 1976; Hartley and Miller 1977).

In 1719 two Frenchmen, unknown to each other, visited the Wichita and left written accounts of their travels (M. Wedel 1981: 25-31). Claude-Charles Dutisne was sent by Jean Baptiste Bienville, Governor-General of Louisiana, to make alliances in anticipation of establishing trade between Louisiana and New Mexico. Dutisne visited two Wichita villages which W. Wedel (1959: 527-533) and M. Wedel (1972-1973: 153-156) suggest were around Neodesha, Wilson County, Kansas, very near the southeastern corner of Kansas. Dutisne was told of several other *Panis* (Wichita) villages to the west-northwest. He variously called the Wichita *pants, panis* and *paniouassa*. Also in 1719, Jean-Baptiste Benard de La Harpe heard of Wichita Indians from the Caddo and he set out to find them. After following his itinerary on the ground, M. Wedel (1974; 1981: 27-30) concluded La Harpe met a large group of natives, mainly

Wichita, on the Arkansas River in Tulsa County, Oklahoma between Tulsa and Haskell. It is not clear from La Harpe's diary that the meeting was at a permanent village, but other lines of evidence indicate that it was at a village of the Tawakoni band of Wichitas. This village would have been about 80 miles nearly straight south of the Wichita village visited the same summer by Dutisne. There seems to have been a general southerly movement of the Wichita during the 1700s so it is possible that by 1719 the Wichita, from near the Smoky Hill River, had moved to southeastern Kansas and northeastern Oklahoma. It is more likely, however, that this entire stretch of the Arkansas River and its tributaries was still Wichita territory in 1719.

In 1832, Chouteau, Ellsworth, and Irving made a 400 mile trip through what is now Oklahoma. Described as "a wide exploring tour, from the Arkansas to the Red [Cimarron] river, including a part of the Pawnee [Pawnee Pict or Wichita] hunting grounds, where no party of white men had as yet penetrated" (Barry 1972: 220-221). The expedition was successful. The brackets are apparently Barry's. In 1834 Colonel Henry Dodge, with about 190 dragoons, visited a Wichita village of nearly 200 grass houses on the north fork of the Red River in Greer County, Oklahoma. Dodge held a general council with Comanches and Kiowas, as well as Wichitas (Barry 1972: 269-270). Greer County is in extreme southwest Oklahoma. In 1838 Paul L. Chouteau (Barry 1972: 305) reported that the "Wee-cha-tah [Wichita], Tow-wac-car-ro, Wacco and Keetz-sah Bands of Pawnee Picts; are corn planters—occupy several permanent villages and reside within the limits of the Comanche Country; which last nation together with the Kaywahs are supplied by them with corn and other products of the earth." The Comanches were reported to "Claim and occupy the country bounded on the North by the Arkansas River, South by the Mexican Settlements, West by the Grand Cordillera, and East by the Cross Timbers" (Berry 1974: 305; Foreman 1933: 148).

From the 1742 journal of Fabry de La Bruyere (M. Wedel 1981: 31-32), we learn that one band of the Wichita, the Mentos, had formerly lived on the Arkansas River above its confluence with the Canadian but had moved to the Canadian and from there, in 1737 or 1738, had moved near the Caddo where they were in 1742. In the same journal other Wichitas, called *panis noirs*, were said to have lived 25 leagues (68 miles) farther up the Arkansas when the Mentos were living on the Arkansas. This could well refer to the village visited by Dutisne in 1719. La Bruyere, in 1742, went south from the Canadian River to the Red where he reported Tavakanas (Tawakoni, the major band of Wichita) living with the Kitsaiches (Kitsai) above the Caddo and Yatasi.

In 1749 [or 1750] a small group of Frenchmen and a German went from New Orleans to the Arkansas Post, located at the mouth of the Arkansas River. In the testimony of one of the group, Felipe de Sandoval (M. Wedel 1981: 10-13), the party went up the Arkansas and after 50 days reached two villages of *Panipiques* or *Jumanos* (Wichitas) who were friendly with both the French and the Comanches. From there the party went on to New Mexico, being conducted to Taos Pueblo by Comanches. In Santa Fe, Sandoval was interrogated by the Spanish and his testimony recorded. M. Wedel makes a good case for the two Wichita villages being the Deer Creek and Bryson-Paddock sites on the west side of the Arkansas River four and six miles south of the Kansas-Oklahoma line.

In 1748 a party of three Frenchmen (Satren, Febre, and Riballo) arrived in New Mexico and were also questioned. Little information on the route that they took after leaving the Arkansas Post was recorded, but they, too, had visited two villages of Panipiques (Wichitas) who were friendly with the French and Comanches. These villages were probably the same two visited by Sandoval. In the testimony of the three Frenchmen, they said that French hunters come to the Panipique to hunt with them. This would fit well with the archeological evidence from the Deer Creek site, where great quantities of bison bone and many large hide scrapers were recovered, along with numerous items of French trade goods. In 1751 there is also mention of a third village on the Arkansas (M. Wedel 1981: 11-13).

In 1759, Don Diego Ortiz Parrilla attacked a Taovayas village on the Red River (Duffield 1965). The site was fortified and in the attack, which was unsuccessful, two cannons were lost and several of Parrilla's men were killed or wounded. There has been speculation as to the exact location of the village. On the basis of archeological investigation Bell, Jelks, and Newcomb (1974: 114) concluded that the Longest Site, on the Oklahoma side of the Red River, nearly straight south of Oklahoma City, was probably the town involved. A fortification ditch was located and the site yielded both native and French materials.

Writing in 1763, Macarty (M. Wedel 1981: 32) attributed the move of the Tehuacanas south to the Red River to their desire to be closer to the French. Their later move, farther south, may be attributed to pressure from other tribes, perhaps Osage. In 1763 they were probably living on the Sabine River where Johnson and Jelks (1958) placed them in 1758-1759.

In the 1770s, Athanase de Mezieres and his associates (Bolton 1914 passim) visited various bands of Wichita who were then living in north central Texas, primarily on the Brazos, Red, and Wichita Rivers. For the most part they were called by their various band or village names, but they were recognized as being of a single nation. During this period they all practiced some horticulture, along with hunting. Also, Skidi Pawnee from eastern Nebraska moved to the Red River, allied themselves with Taovayas, and seem not to have returned to the Platte River area until the early 1800s.

In 1786 Pedro Vial (Loomis and Nasatir 1967: 268-285; John 1975: 719-727) set out from Bexar (San Antonio), to find a route to Santa Fe. He was to go by the way of the Taovayas and Wichitas, a few of whom had recently stolen some horses from the Spanish at Bexar. It is not possible to reconstruct his route exactly, for Vial wandered around a great deal; he did not make contact then with the Taovayas and Wichitas. He did, however, come to a Tawakoni village somewhere in north-central Texas, where he stayed for seven weeks, recovering from an illness. Thereafter, he pressed on to the Red River and the villages of the Taovayas and Wichitas. Vial's trip from Santa Fe to the Jumanos (Wichitas), and on to San Antonio de Bexar in 1788, is chronicled in diaries kept by Santiago Fernandez and Francisco Fragoso (Loomis and Nasatir 1967: 316-368). The party essentially followed the Red River, which was then called the Rio Blanco, starting at its head waters west of Canyon, Texas. All along the Rio Blanco numerous Comanches were met until the party was within about 60 miles of the first Jumano (Wichita) villages, located about 62 miles east of Wichita Falls, Texas. Newcomb and Field (in Bell, Jelks and Newcomb 1974: 286) suggest that the villages they visited were in the vicinity of Spanish Fort, Texas. Little detail is given, but it seems quite certain that these Jumanos were Taovayas.

In 1834, an expedition under Colonel Henry Dodge visited and described a Wichita village on the North Branch of the Red River in southwestern Oklahoma: "situated immediately under mountains of granite." Without doubt, these are the Granite Mountains close to Granite, Oklahoma. The village consisted of 200 grass houses and the Wichita raised an abundance of corn, squash and melons, and they had a good supply of dried meat. In 1852, Randolph Marcy apparently passed by the same spot, but made no mention of a village (Foreman 1937: 37). In 1835, a treaty was made to conclude a peace among the Wichita, Comanche, eastern tribes and the United States Government. At this time, the Wichita became officially known as Wichita. In 1834, a Wichita village was noted as being located near Lugert, Oklahoma (Bell, Jelks and Newcomb 1974: 323-324). In 1841, George Kendall reported that the *Wichetaws* and *Towyash* lived on the north side of the Red River in the Wichita Mountains, and the *Wocanies, Kechies,* and *Waeos* were on the Brasos River, about 100 miles above Comanche Peak (Bell, Jelks and Newcomb 1974: 324-325). By then the population had been greatly depleted by smallpox and Texans' raids. In December 1835, Major Chouteau went up the Red River in an attempt to make contact with the Kiowa. He met some bands of Tawakoni and Waco along the river, probably in what is now Tillman County, southwestern Oklahoma. They were returning to occupy some country from which they had been driven by the Osage. They intended to plant corn in the spring (Foreman 1926: 224). Presumably the Wichita had a village near where Chouteau met the Tawakoni and Waco, whom he also visited.

In 1852, Marcy passed two old native villages which, according to one of his hunters, had been occupied by Wichitas and Keechis. They were abandoned for only two years; several lodges were still standing and corn fields were noted nearby. These were at the location of the future Fort Sill, just north of Lawton, Oklahoma (Foreman 1937: 116). Presumably the Wichita had moved to this village from the one near Granite, Oklahoma where they were reported in 1834. Marcy continued on and came to two villages, one of Wacos and one of Wichitas, on Rush Creek near the future location of Rush Springs, Oklahoma. They still raised a variety of garden produce and lived in conical grass houses that Marcy described in detail. There were 42 Wichita lodges housing nearly the entire surviving Wichita population of about 500 individuals. The Waco village, with 20 lodges, was like that of the Wichita and about a mile away (Foreman 1937: 124-126). In 1857, about 900 Wichita and 300 Kichai who were along Rush Creek were said to be living in a single village and were intermarried. And to the north, on the Canadian River, not far from present-day Oklahoma City, there were 300 Waco and Tawakoni (Foreman 1933: 269).

During 1854, a reservation was established in Texas, on the Brazos River near the mouth of the Clear Fork, some 60 miles south of Wichita Falls, Texas. Here some Waco and Tawakoni, among other non-Wichita natives, were settled and soon various Wichita groups were attracted to the reservation. Nearby Europeans became hostile. Skirmishes ensued and the Wichitas were removed from Texas. In 1855, an area was provided in Indian Territory (Oklahoma) for the Wichita and others. In 1859, a reservation for the Wichita was established on the Washita River at the site of an old Kichai village (Bell, Jelks and Newcomb 1974: 295-300). In 1861, at the outbreak of the Civil War, Union forces left Oklahoma, leaving the Wichitas and other tribes unprovided for. In 1862, the Wichitas moved north into Kansas, first to near Belmont, and then to Wichita. In 1867, the Wichitas were moved back into Indian Territory (Bell, Jelks and Newcomb 1974: 301-303).

In summary, the Wichitas appear to have migrated in a circle during the thousand years of their reconstructed and recorded history. It seems likely that they had at least some of their roots in the Middle Ceramic complexes along the Washita River of Western Oklahoma and that by late prehistoric times they had moved to what is now south-central Kansas. At the dawn of recorded history they expanded northward along the Arkansas River to the Smoky Hill River in central Kansas. By the middle of the 1700s the center of their territory shifted south to southeastern Kansas and into northeastern Oklahoma. Well before the end of the 1700s, they were centered in southeastern Oklahoma and northeastern Texas. Soon they were forced west by Osage pressure, to north-central Texas. Additional pressures, primarily from Texan settlers in the early and mid-1800s, resulted in their moving into southwestern Oklahoma. Except for a few years during the Civil War when they took refuge in Kansas, the Wichita have remained on a reservation in Caddo County, Oklahoma through which flows the Washita River.

CHAPTER FOUR

THE PAWNEES

To the east and northeast of the northern Central High Plains were the Pawnee who, along with the Arikara, Wichita and Caddo, formed a more or less solid block of Caddoan speakers extending from South Dakota into Texas. They were essentially the westernmost horticulturalists of the plains during the historic period. The immediate ancestors of the Pawnee, known archaeologically as the Lower Loup people, were descended from at least some of the Upper Republican people who dominated much of the central plains in late prehistoric times. Caddoan occupation of the plains probably extends back several thousand years, although, from time-to-time, adverse climatic conditions appear to have caused substantial population reductions or even temporary abandonment of parts of the area. In the mid-1700s the continuous block of Caddoans was finally broken when the Arikara moved farther north and were replaced in South Dakota by Siouan speakers.

The ethnohistory of the Pawnee has been discussed by a number of authors. Strong (1935), drawing heavily on cartographic evidence, provided a brief summary as background for the understanding of the archaeology of Nebraska. W. Wedel (1936, 1938, 1979), Grange (1968) and M. Wedel (1979) explored the subject more thoroughly. Although the Pawnee villages lay just beyond the Central High Plains, their ethnohistory will be considered here since they were the end product of a long cultural development in the central plains and continued to be a power in the area.

By about A.D. 1500 the immediate ancestors of the Pawnee lived in permanent earth lodge villages along the Loup River in east-central Nebraska. By the late 1600s the Pawnee were known as such with various spellings of the name. Coronado's party of 1541 (Winship 1896; Hammond and Rey 1940) did not reach Pawnee territory, but the people of "Harahey" mentioned in the chronicles of the expedition were apparently Pawnee. They were said to have a culture similar to that of the people of Quivira, the Wichita. In an article by Mildred Wedel (1979) dealing with the pre-1800 ethnohistory of the Wichita, Pawnee and Arikara, she points out that the Pawnee are frequently mentioned and were apparently quite numerous before 1800, but that their villages were not described by eyewitnesses until after that date. Presumably much of the information received about the Pawnees by the French came from the *voyageurs*, often illiterate traders, who were concerned with fur trading and exploration. Some Pawnee also traveled east or were

taken east as slaves. Since the Pawnee were up the Platte and Loup Rivers and thus away from the Missouri River, many explorers and traders did not visit them. From 1673, when Jacques Marquette and Louis Jolliet made their historic trip down the Mississippi River, showing the Pawnee in the correct location on their maps, references to the Pawnee became quite common. According to M. Wedel (1979: 192) it was not until 1701 that the French recognized two groups of the Pawnee, the Panimaha (Skidi) and the Panis (South Band Pawnee or Pawnee proper). In 1775, the Republican, or Kitkehaki, band of the Pawnee was recognized and in 1794 the Chaui, or Grand, and the Pitahauerat, or Tappage, bands were distinguished. The Skidi, or Skiri, were also commonly called Pawnee Loups by the French, Lobos by the Spanish, and the Wolves by English speakers. During the 1700s, the estimates of Pawnee population and of the number of their villages varied markedly. Brugge (1965: 186-187) found in the church records of New Mexico notations for the baptism or burial of many Pawnees, starting in 1702 and extending to the mid-1800s. Most of these were at parishes along the Rio Grande from Santa Fe north.

About 1770 the Skidi Pawnee moved from their homeland on the Loup River, in eastern Nebraska, to the Red river in northeastern Texas. There they joined the Taovayas band of the Wichita, their linguistic relatives (Bolton 1914: I 202). The Skidi remained there until about 1800 when they returned to their former homeland. This movement may, in part, account for the Skidi's reputation as wanderers. By the late 1700s at least one Pawnee village was established in northern Kansas, but the territory soon contracted back to east central Nebraska.

The 1739 trip of the Mallet brothers, Pierre and Paul, is an especially interesting milestone in the history of plains-southwest relationships. The brothers set out from a Pawnee village on the Platte River, passed near the future location of Lincoln, Nebraska, reached the Arkansas River not far west of Great Bend, Kansas, and then followed essentially the route of the future Santa Fe Trail into Santa Fe. Interestingly enough, for the latter part of their journey, they had an Arikara guide. The Mallet brothers were apparently the first Europeans to go from the Missouri River to New Mexico by this route although earlier Spanish explorers had followed sections of this same trail, the western most part of which was to become the Santa Fe Trail.

In 1720, Antonio Valverde, Governor of New Mexico, sent Pedro de Villasur with a large party, including the best plainsmen of New Mexico, plus native auxiliaries, to the Platte River to determine the extent of French activity in the area. The party went out by the way of the Cuartelejo Apaches, from whom were recruited additional auxiliaries. Although only the last few pages of the expedition diary survived (Thomas 1935: 133-137), it is quite apparent that contact was made at the confluence of the Loup and Platte Rivers, not at the forks of the Platte as some authors have suggested. The diary describes a native village whose location and setting matches that of the Bellwood Pawnee site (25 BU 2), near Bellwood, Nebraska, which is dated at 1685-1777 and 1795 by Grange (1968: 27, 130). The earlier Lower Loup (proto-historic Paw'ee) occupation is of the correct time period and no other known site has both the right setting and date. The Villasur party was thoroughly defeated by the Pawnees among whom may have been some Oto and/or Missouri. In a skin painting that apparently depicts the Villasur Massacre there are a number of individuals dressed like Frenchmen, others dressed as Spaniards and natives in several styles of dress (Hotz 1960, 1970). This massacre ended any real Spanish contention for the territory along the Missouri River and it was another 75 to 85 years before New Mexicans attempted to enter this area again, which in the meantime, was dominated by the French.

In 1720, Felix Martinez testified, in connection with the Villasur incident, that the Pawnee lived in four or five settlements on the river Jesus Maria (Platte River) some 200 leagues (550 miles) from Santa Fe. He reported that there were French among the Pawnee and that there were no horses in their country. The French settlements, however, were thought to be very distant from the Pawnee villages (Thomas 1935: 170-172). Also in November 1720, one Bartolome Garduno testified that the distance from Santa Fe to the Pawnee was 225 leagues (615 miles), a distance that is essentially accurate although some of his distances between intermediate points are quite inaccurate (Thomas 1935: 173). In the fragment of the Villasur diary that has survived (Thomas 1935: 133-137), the length of the journey from Santa Fe to the Platte River was estimated at about 300 leagues (820 miles), five days before the massacre, at which time the Spanish were already close to the Pawnee. Even considering that the route was not a straight line, this distance is excessive. Valverde, writing in 1720, gives the distance from Santa Fe to El Cuartelejo as 130 leagues (354 miles) and from El Cuartelejo to the Pawnee as 70 leagues (191 miles) (Thomas 1935: 155). The 70 league distance is probably more accurate than the distance of 50 leagues commonly given, but even 70 is short if the distance was from the assumed location of the principal village of

El Cuartelejo, in Scott County, Kansas, to the Pawnee villages on the lower Loup River, near its mouth. The 130-league distance would be reasonable for the distance from Santa Fe to Scott County, Kansas.

In 1792-1793 Pedro Vial made a round trip from Santa Fe to St. Louis. His diary was edited by Loomis and Nasatir (1967), who suggested that Vials' league equaled 2.6 miles. On his return trip Vial went up the Missouri River to the mouth of the Little Nemaha River and from there was guided by a group of Pawnees to their village. The reconstruction of this route (Gunnerson 1984) takes him to a known Pawnee village just west of Republic, Kansas. Vial's daily distances, and his evening camps according to this reconstruction, are as follows: On the 12th he traveled southwest 4 leagues (11 miles) to a branch to either Muddy or Little Muddy Creek near Stella, Nebraska (not a branch of the Little Nemaha as Vial believed). On the 13th, is 6 leagues (16 miles) would have taken him to the North Branch of the Big Nemaha, below Table Rock, Nebraska. On the 14th he traveled 7 leagues (19 miles), again to the southwest to Johnson Creek, south of Burchard, Nebraska. The rest of his trip was to the west and all south of the Nebraska-Kansas line. On the 15th his 7 leagues (19 miles) would have taken him to the Big Blue River near Oketo. On the 16th he traveled 5 leagues (13 miles) and arrived on the Little Blue River about 1.5 miles above Hanover. The 17th took him 6 leagues (15 miles) to about the mouth of Salt Creek. On the 18th he apparently followed Mill Creek to 5 miles west of Haddam. On the 19th he saw a high hill, probably the ridge 2.4 miles north of Bellville, while traveling 4 leagues (10 miles) to Riley Creek. Then on September 20th, he continued on for 5 leagues (13 miles) to a Pawnee village near Republic, Kansas.

A straight line distance from the mouth of the Little Nemaha to this Pawnee village is about 119 miles and as reconstructed is 129 miles, or 50 leagues — Vial calculated 49 leagues. The straight line distance from the mouth of the Little Nemaha to a known Pawnee village near Red Cloud, Nebraska, the only likely alternative, is 144 miles or 55 leagues. Vial continued on to Santa Fe, taking a delegation of Pawnees with him. From the Pawnee village, his route as reconstructed, took him across the Arkansas River, just east of Dodge City, then diagonally across the panhandles of Oklahoma and Texas. He hit the Canadian River just before it leaves New Mexico, and then proceeded nearly straight west into Santa Fe.

There is some suggestion that Pedro Vial went to the Pawnee again in 1794 but documentation is very scanty (Loomis and Nasatir 1967: 421-423). In 1804 Vial, with a small party, went from Santa Fe to Pawnee village(s?) on the

Platte River. The diary of this trip has recently come to light and has been translated by Nasatir (1974: 114-119). A probable reconstruction of his route is: Vial went from Santa Fe to Taos and across the mountains east to near Rayado. From there he followed the foothills northeast, crossed Raton mesa about 20 miles east of Raton, New Mexico and proceeded down Smith Canyon (his canyon of "Casa Colorado") to the Purgatory River. In turn, he followed it to near the Arkansas River. He crossed that river near Lamar, Colorado and traveled north, crossing the Big Sandy, the Smoky Hill (his "Rio de los Canzes"), and branches of the Republican near their heads, while gradually swinging northeast. Near the southwest corner of Nebraska he came to, and began to follow, the Republican River which he called a branch of the Rio de los Canzes. When he was near Franklin, Nebraska, he cut northeast, reaching the Platte River some 22 miles east of Kearney, Nebraska. He followed the Platte 81 miles to a Pawnee village near the mouth of the Loup River. No detailed description of the village is given but it is probably either the Bellwood or Linwood site, each named after a nearby town in Nebraska and described by Grange (1968: 19, 20). The Vial party stayed among the Pawnee for two weeks and were well treated. Apparently there were two bands of Pawnees represented, for in addition to the main group, called Pananas, there were "two captains of the Panis, which is the same nation and the same language." Also present were two Oto captains and about 20 Frenchmen (Nasatir 1974: 117-118).

In the cover letter that accompanied a copy of Vial's diary sent by Rafael Chacon to Nemesio Salcedo, Chacon states that Vial's trip was to the Rio Chato "where the pueblos of the Panana and Abajoses people are located" (Nasatir 1974: 113). The identity of the Abajoses is uncertain, but they could have been the Oto, who are mentioned in the diary, or they might be the Skidi band of Pawnees who, by then, may have returned from their long stay among the Wichita.

On Vial's return trip he was accompanied by eleven young Pawnee men and one of their Chiefs, a Captain Caigie. When the party reached what is thought to be the confluence of Smith Canyon and the Purgatoire, they met a party of about 100 Comanches returning by the same route. The Pawnees accompanied the Comanches to their rancherias where they stayed for three days. Upon reaching Santa Fe some of the Pawnees were given Spanish medals and other gifts. There is reference to Spanish medals and patents having previously been given to Indians from the Missouri River area (Nasatir 1974: 117-118). On October 11, 1805, Governor Joaquin Alencaster, of New Mexico, proposed to again send Pedro Vial on an expedition to the Pawnees in an attempt to strengthen Spanish-Pawnee relationships (Loomis and Nasatir 1967: 428-438) and to learn what he could of the Lewis and Clark expedition up the Missouri River. In his directions to Vial, it was indicated that he might find Pawnees on the Platte River near its mouth, on the Kansa or its tributaries, and perhaps even on the Arkansas. The Pawnee, Lobos (Skidi), and Otos are mentioned together, suggesting again that their proximity to one another was known. With Vial, this time, was a large party, including an interpreter, Chalvert, who knew the Pawnee. This party went from Santa Fe to Taos, across the Sangre de Cristo mountains to the east and then took a near straight course to the confluence of the Purgatory and Arkansas Rivers. There the expedition was stopped, thoroughly routed and forced to turn back by a group of unidentified Indians or possibly Anglo-Americans. The next spring Vial and Chalvert set out on another expedition to the Pawnee, but it, too, was cut short when their men deserted (Loomis and Nasatir 1967: 446-447).

The next Spanish attempt to make contact with the Pawnee was successful. In the spring of of 1806 Lieutenant Facundo Melgares, with some 100 individuals, was sent to Santa Fe, where he added an additional 400 to his party. He went east from Santa Fe, followed the Red River (Canadian) for a way and then cut northeast to the Arkansas and on to a Pawnee village on the Republican River (Loomis and Nasatir 1967: 445). Melgares presented the Pawnees with medals and a Spanish flag. Within a few weeks after Melgares' visit to this Pawnee village, Captain Zebulon M. Pike arrived there and persuaded, with difficulty, the Pawnee to replace the Spanish flag with the American thus generally restoring good relations. Pike then followed the trail left by the Melgares party to the Arkansas River, where he went west into the mountains where it rose west of Canon City, Colorado. He was captured by the Spanish in the San Luis Valley and taken to Santa Fe (Jackson 1966).

The location of the "Pike-Pawnee" village on the Republican River has long been a subject of controversy. Early in the present century historians in Kansas concluded that a Pawnee archeological site near Republic, Kansas was the Pike-Pawnee village and erected a monument so proclaiming it. But the topography around this site did not match Pike's precise description, thus leaving doubt as to the identification. Mr. A.T. Hill, later to become Director of the Nebraska State Historical Society Museum, set out to find a more likely site, which he did near Red Cloud, Nebraska. This site, known as the Hill Site, is now generally accepted as the village visited by Pike in the summer of 1806 (Wedel 1936: 32-36).

Two years earlier, in 1804, Lewis and Clark had camped near the mouth of the Platte River on their trip up the Missouri in their tabulations, Lewis and Clark (1904: 86-87) recorded three bands of Pawnees: the "Grand Pani" who live on the south side of the Platte River 30 leagues (82 miles) above the mouth and "hunt on the heads of the Kanzes, and its NW waters and high up on the Platt;" the "Pani Loup or Skee-e-ree [Skidi]....40 leagues [110 miles] above the Panis on the right of the R. Loup which empties into the Platt 8 Lg [22 miles] above the Panis, they hunt on the rivers Platt & Loup above their village", and the Pani Republicans whose "village is with the Pani on the River Platt, they hunt on a branch of the Kanzus called the Republican fork, and near the Kanzes river." Apparently by then the Republican band was split with some living on the Republican River and some on the Platte. Lewis and Clark either did not learn of the Tappage or simply lumped them with another band. Wedel (1936: 29-31, 17) identifies the Grand Pawnee village as the Linwood Site and the Skidi village as probably the Palmer Site; the two sites are named after nearby towns in Nebraska.

In 1811 Major Sibley visited several Pawnee villages. The Skidi village he noted is thought by Wedel to be the Palmer Site and that area occupied by the Republican and Grand Bands as the Horse Creek Site, located about 9 miles southwest of Fullerton, Nebraska (Wedel 1936: 17, 25, 36). This may represent a return to the Loup River area of all or part of the Republican Pawnees from the Republican River drainage. Presumably the Republican Band occupation of the Hill site, near Red Cloud, Nebraska, lasted from about 1775 until 1815 and that of the Kansas Monument site, near Republic, Kansas, from about 1775 to 1800 and/or 1821 to 1833 (Grange 1968: 18). In 1825 Jedediah Smith and some 60 men left St. Louis for the Rocky Mountains. In January 1826 they stayed for a while in a Republican Band Pawnee village on the Republican River while the Pawnees were on a hunt. When they returned he paid them for the stored corn that his party had eaten. Barry (1972: 130-132) identifies this billage as the one in Republic County, Kansas. Even after the abandonment of their villages on the Republican River, the Pawnee continued to hunt in western Kansas and eastern Colorado. In 1822, the Hugh Glenn-Jacob Fowler party met a group of 400 to 500 Pawnees along the Arkansas near Larned, in southwestern Kansas. With these Pawnee was at least one Comanche chief (Coues 1970: 125). During the 1830s and 1840s, Pawnees, in groups of a hundred or more, frequently appeared along the Arkansas River in southeastern Colorado and southwestern Kansas, raiding and fighting with members of various other tribes (Lavender 1972).

In 1835, Charles Murray traveled wih a Pawnee summer hunting party made up of Grand, Tappage, Republican and, for awhile, Skidi and Oto. He provides interesting ethnographic detail, including some on temporary summer tents, which differ from the standard plains tipi (Murray 1839 I: 284). These semicircular structures had small curved poles driven into the ground on the circumference and four larger posts set vertically across the straight front, which was sometimes left open. Such structures might be identifiable archaeologically. While the hunting party was apparently between the Republican and Smoky Hill Rivers, a small party of Arikaras raided it and stole horses. A few days later there was a skirmish between the Pawnees and a group of Delaware and Shawnee hunters on their way from a village, near Fort Levenworth, to the Rocky Mountains. Even though they were not hostile, the Pawnees thought that they had no right to hunt on the buffalo plains (Murray 1839 I: 414-417).

Meanwhile, the Pawnee earth lodge villages in eastern Nebraska were being visited more and more frequently by travelers who left written accounts. In early June, 1820, an exploring party under Major Stephen H. Long set out from Council Bluffs, Iowa on a trip up the Platte River to the Rocky Mountains, returning by way of the Arkansas and Canadian Rivers (Bell 1947: 103 ff). The first Pawnee village reached by the party, probably the Horse Creek site on the north side of the Loup River near Fullerton, Nebraska, was occupied by the Grand Pawnee (Wedel 1936: 36-37). The next day the party visited a Republican Band village on the same side of the Loup River and about 3.7 miles upstream from the first. Wedel (1936: 38) identifies this village as the Cottonwood Creek Site, near Palmer, Nebraska. Another 4 miles up the Loup was a Loup (Skidi) Band village, probably the Palmer Site (Wedel 1936: 26). The Tappage may then have been living with the Republican band at the Cottonwood Creek Site, northeast of Palmer, where they were found by Irving (1955) in 1833.

When, in 1833, John T. Irving (1955: 119 ff) visited the Pawnee for about 10 days, he found Mr. Ellsworth and Major Dougherty. They in turn helped introduce Irving to the various chiefs. Irving mentions four villages, each of a different band of Pawnee. Wedel (1936: 25-38) has identified these villages with their band affiliations as follows: the Clarks Site, southeast of Clarks, Nebraska, as Grand; the Palmer Site as Skidi (Loup); the Horse Creek Site as Republican; and the Cottonwood Creek Site as Tappage (cf. Irving 1955: 141 n for different identifications). The Clarks site was on the Platte while the other three were on the Loup River; the most distant villages would have been about 25 miles from one another. Irving (1955: 130) learned that the Grand Pawnee Village (the Clarks Site) had recently been rebuilt after being burned by Delawares. During the time that Irving was at the village of the Grand Pawnee, Ellsworth negotiated a treaty with the various Pawnee chiefs in which they agreed to give up all territory south of the Platte River and live on the Loup.

Irving visited the Pawnee villages and recorded a great deal of information about the customs and behavior of the Pawnee. For example, he learned that shortly before his arrival, the Skidi had planned to sacrifice a captured Cheyenne woman to the Morning Star. Major Dougherty, the Pawnee Agent, had succeeded in stopping the sacrifice but while he was conducting the Cheyenne victim from the village, a Pawnee Soldier Chief, who had been incensed by the prevention of the sacrifice, shot the captive, who was, in turn, torn to pieces by an angry Pawnee crowd (Irving 1955: 184-188). The sacrifice to the Morning Star, apparently a long-standing tradition among the Skidi, and part of an elaborate star lore held by all Pawnee, may have had its roots in the southwest, perhaps as far south as the Aztecs, where human sacrifice was common. The last attempted Skidi sacrifice was in 1817 when a young Pawnee chief, Pitalesharo, freed a female captive from the scaffolding to which she was bound and returned her to her own tribe.

John Dunbar and a Mr. Allis were Presbyterian missionaries to the Pawnee, arriving in the fall of 1834 (Dunbar 1835, 1880). Allis went to the Pawnee Loup and Dunbar to the Grand Pawnee. Wedel identifies the Loup (Skidi) village as the Palmer site and the location of the mission for the Grand as near the Plum Creek site, about 8 miles southwest of Genoa, Nebraska (Wedel 1936: 32; Grange 1968: 23). Dunbar apparently first went briefly to a Grand Pawnee village on the south side of the Platte River "about 120 miles" from the mouth, which would match the location of the Clarks Site (Dunbar 1835: 346). Dunbar, who lived and traveled with the Pawnee for several years, provides a great deal of excellent ethnographic information.

In 1835, Colonel Henry Dodge (1836) traveled up the Platte and South Platte Rivers to the Rocky Mountains, then south to the Arkansas River which he followed eastward on his return to Fort Leavenworth. Going up the south side of the Platte River he came to a Grand Pawnee village about 80 miles above an Oto village that he had passed. This is probably the Clarks Site that Irving had visited two years before (Wedel 1936: 19). Dodge mentions the other Pawnee bands but does not give the locations of their villages. When Dodge was among the Pawnees, he wanted to meet with the Arikaras who, at that time, were living with the Skidi Pawnee on the Loup River. At first the Arikaras were afraid to meet with him but they finally did, catching up with him close to the forks of the Platte River, near the location

of North Platte, Nebraska. Later, when Dodge was with a band of Cheyennes on the Arkansas River near the Colorado-Kansas line, a group of Arikaras and Skidi arrived on the scene to make peace with the Cheyennes and all agreed to hunt together a few months later. Dodge noted that at one time the Arikaras had lived with the Cheyennes, presumably after they had been displaced from the Missouri River by the Sioux. The Skidi ("Pawnee Mokow") apparently returned south in 1837 and attacked the Wichita and the "Pa-do-kay's" (Foreman 1926: 234, 238).

In 1844, Lieutenant J. Henry Carlton (1943: 64), and five companies of Dragoons under the command of Major Clifton Wharton, visited the Pawnee, who were living in four villages. According to Carlton, the Grand Pawnee were living at what Wedel (1936: 31) has identified as the Clarks Site. The Republican band was situated 9 miles farther up the Platte River and was also on the south side at what is probably the Hordville Site, described by Grange (1968: 20). The Loup (Skidi) were living 18 miles to the north, on the north bank of the Loup River, probably at the site near Fullerton that Wedel (1936: 27) identifies as having been occupied by the Skidi from 1842 until 1846. The fourth site, occupied by the "Tepage," also on the north bank of the Loup River, was nine miles upstream from the Skidi village. This location fits the Horse Creek site, although Dunbar (Wedel 1936: 36) stated that it was a Republican band village abandoned in 1842. Carlton (1943) provides considerable ethnographic information, including such things as details on earthlodges and burial practices that would be of special interest to archeologists. Carlton (1943: 107) estimated the population of the Pawnee at about 6500 including 1000 warriors. He recounts an attack by three to four hundred Sioux warriors on a Pawnee village the previous year (June 1843) in which over half of the lodges were burned. This village, situated on the Loup River, between two tributaries, and included the houses of the tribe's missionary, farmer and blacksmith on the other side of the tributary to the east. It has been identified as the Plum Creek site. It is also known as the Burnt Village and the Mission Village (Wedel 1936: 32; Grange 1968: 23). Presumably it had been occupied by Grands, Republicans, and Tappage (Wedel 1936: 32), and survivors of the Sioux attack who were moved to various other villages (Carlton 1943: 109). At least a substantial portion of the Pawnees living there were of the Republican Band, since Capote-Bleu, a chief of that band (Irving 1955: 123 n), was killed in the attack while leading the defense of his village. Apparently most of the surviving Republican Band Pawnee that lived at Burnt Village moved to a village near Hordville, Nebraska, apparently occupied only briefly in 1844 (Grange 1968: 18).

In 1851, two Moravian missionaries, Gottlieb Oehler and David Smith (1914), made a brief visit to the Pawnee who, by then, were apparently living in only two villages, both on the south side of the Platte. The lower village, a few miles above the mouth of the Elkhorn, identified by Wedel (1936: 28) as the McClaine site, was occupied by the Skidi. At the upper village, 25 miles farther upstream, Oehler and Smith met chiefs of the Grand, Republican and Tappage bands of the Pawnee. The distance is right for this to be the Linwood site, which had a second phase of occupation at this time. Wedel (1936: 22) accepts it as the upper village even though normally the Skidi lived west of the other bands. Grange (1968: 18, 24) attributes the late occupation of the Linwood Site to the Grand, and the occupation of the McClaine site to the Skidi and Tappage while considering the Leshara Site as essentially part of the Mcclaine site with Skidi or Grand and Republican occupants. Of significance is that all of the Pawnee were concentrated in two villages about 25 miles apart. Oehler and Smith were fortunate to have the services of Allis as their interpreter since he maintained a government school for Pawnee children and

he had been in residence for some time. It is interesting that at the time Oehler and Smith (1914: 16) were with the Pawnee (in May 1851), a government employee and his interpreter arrived to invite the Pawnee to come to a council at Fort Laramie the following September. The purpose of the council, discussed elsewhere, was to reach agreement on the boundaries of hunting territories for the various tribes that hunted in the Central High Plains.

The last Pawnee tribal hunt (in 1873) ended in disaster when the Pawnee were attacked and defeated by a group of Dakota Sioux near Trenton, Nebraska. The continuing threat of the Sioux probably had much to do with the Pawnees' willingness to leave eastern Nebraska where their ancestors had lived for untold hundreds or thousands of years. In response to the 1805 treaty of Table Rock, all of the Pawnee moved to Genoa, Nebraska where the Government established a reservation headquarters. The Pawnee remained at Genoa until 1876, when the last of them moved to a reservation in Oklahoma. Some had moved to Oklahoma even as early as 1874 (Wedel 1936: 22-23).

CHAPTER FIVE

THE UTES

The Utes had probably been in southern Colorado, including the drainage of the Rio Grande, since late prehistoric, or earlier, times. The ancestors of these Shoshonean speaking people occupied the Great Basin for several thousand years. After the Utes acquired horses, they sometimes moved out of the mountains onto the high plains, perhaps first in the company of their linguistic relatives, the Comanche. The Comanche went on to become much more of a power than did the Utes. The Utes that occupied the Central High Plains in southern Colorado and northern New Mexico, were probably all of the Capote and Moache bands, sometimes called the Taos Utes because of their proximity to this town.

The Utes were known to the Spanish since at least the early 1600s, but they had been no major threat except for stealing a few horses. In 1694, after the reconquest of New Mexico by Diego de Vargas, a Spanish party under Vargas went to Taos, which was abandoned at the Spaniard's approach, and stole a great deal of corn. Rather than risking attack in the mountainous area around Picuris Pueblo, the Spanish chose to cross the Rio Grande north of Taos, in Ute territory, because the Utes had always been friendly with the Spanish (Espinosa 1942: 193; D. Gunnerson 1974: 118). In 1706 Ulibarri was forced to remain in Taos for two days because of an expected attack by Utes and Comanches. But it did not materialize. A few days later Ulibarri met Penxayes Apaches near Two Buttes, Colorado who hastened to join their relatives, the Carlanas, due to an anticipated attack from Utes and Comanches (Thomss 1935: 61-65).

By 1719 the Utes stole enough horses and committed enough other depredations that the New Mexicans held a council of war and decided to take military action against the Utes (Thomas 1935: 99-133; Gunnerson 1984), and the Comanches with whom they were allied. In the fall of 1719 a war party under the leadership of Antonio de Valverde left Taos, crossed east over the mountains to about Rayado, traveled through the Jicarilla settlements in the foothills near Cimarron, and crossed Raton Pass into the vicinity of Trinidad, Colorado where they were joined by Carlana Apache auxiliaries. From there the Spanish went north along the foothills to near Colorado Springs where they headed northeast until they were about 30 miles from Colorado Springs. There they turned southeast and, near River Bend, reached the Big Sandy, which Valverde followed until he turned south, reaching the Arkansas River about 10 miles east of Las Animas, Colorado. At about the time Valverde

was in the Trinidad area, he sent out spies in the hope of locating the Utes and Comanches, but none were found, only their trails. From the time he crossed Raton Pass, until he reached the Arkansas River, he was within Ute and Comanche territory which was north of the Carlana Apaches and west of the Cuartelejo Apaches.

Utes and Comanches continued to attack the Jicarillas across the Sangre de Cristos from Taos and by 1748 had forced these Apaches to move west into the Rio Grande valley near Taos Pueblo (Thomas 1935: 193-219). The Utes and Comanches continued as a threat to Spanish, as well as, Apache settlement. In the middle of the 1700s the Comanches and Utes became enemies . The Moache Utes were allied with the Jicarilla (Thomas 1940: 114-115; D. Gunnerson 1974: 219, 230); a relationship that has never really terminated.

In 1779 Governor Juan Bautista de Anza led an expedition from Santa Fe into southeastern Colorado to punish the Comanches (Thomas 1932). He stayed west of the Rio Grande until he was near the present Colorado-New Mexico line. Three days earlier his party was joined by 200 Ute and Apache allies. The Utes that accompanied him were said to reside near the source of the Rio Grande which was in a "great swamp." This would be the San Luis Valley. De Anza mentions coming to "a pleasant pond named San Luis." Here, the previous summer, "a large number of Comanches attacked a greater force of Utes who were camped there with their families" (Thomas 1932: 127). From the San Luis Valley, de Anza crossed the mountains east to the upper Rio de Napestle (Arkansas River). After crossing the Arkansas, he traveled 25 leagues (68 miles) north along the foothills where he attacked and thoroughly defeated a large camp of Comanches. This would have been near the location of Castle Rock, Colorado. De Anza then turned south, and at the Arkansas River he met a smaller group of the same band of Comanches who, along with their primary chief, Cuerno Verde, were returning from New Mexico. This group of Comanches was soundly defeated with Cuerno Verde and several other leaders being killed. Before this second encounter, some of the Utes with de Anza returned to their land. Shortly before reaching Taos, the remaining Utes also returned. In 1786 peace was made between the New Mexicans, the Utes and the Comanches. Although the Utes did not like the idea of the Spanish being at peace with the Comanches, their traditional enemies, this peace lasted for a quarter of a century (Thomas 1932: 66-83). Whereas the Comanches became the dominant tribe on the southern plains during the last half of the 1700s, the Utes never became a major power there. For the most part the Utes restricted their activities to the mountainous areas and foothills of south-central Colorado and northeastern New Mexico, until they joined other Ute bands in western Colorado and eastern Utah.

Zebulon M. Pike, in 1810, reported that Utes, along with Kiowas, were to the north of the Comanches, which would put them somewhere in northeastern Colorado. It is not clear which band of Utes these were, but they probably were not Moache. In 1820 the Long expedition, following southward along the foothills of the Rockies and east along the Arkansas and Canadian rivers, reported several different tribes, but Utes were not among them (Bell 1957).

In 1853, John W. Gunnison's party learned that a year before some Utah Indians had raided a Mexican farmstead, which had fortifications. This occurred at the foot of the mountains on the Greenhorn River, about 31 miles southwest of present Pueblo, Colorado (Beckwith 1855: 33). The same report indicated that Utahs [Utes] occasionally got as far east as present Las Animas, Colorado.

Colonel Dodge (1836: 22-23), who explored along the foothills of the Rocky Mountains between the headwaters of the Platte and the Arkansas in 1835, noted that although the area was primarily that of the Arapahos and Cheyennes, it was "frequented by large parties of Blackfeet, Crows, Snakes and sometimes Eutaus [Utes], who live upon the waters of the Rio del Norte [Rio Grande] and come over the mountain passes to steal horses from the Arepahas and Cheyennes." In the late 1840s and early 1850s the territory of the Utes was in the mountainous areas north and northwest of the New Mexican settlements along the Rio Grande, that is, from the San Luis valley westward (Abel 1915: 7, 32, Map 2, Map 3). Calhoun, however, in 1849, found Utes among the Indians at the Santa Fe Trail crossing of the Arkansas, near today's Garden City, Kansas. Here many Indians waited for the return of [Thomas] Fitzpatrick, their agent, from whom they expected to receive presents (Abel 1915: 18).

W. H. Emory (1848: 12-13) in the diary he kept while on the Kearney Expedition, which essentially followed the Santa Fe Trail, mentioned various tribes in western Kansas and eastern Colorado, but the Utes were not included. After he crossed Raton Pass and was between Mora [New Mexico] and the Ocate River, he met two Mexicans from Mora who were checking on a report that Eutaws [Utes] were in the area. This tribe, along with Navahos and Apaches, were said to sometimes raid Mexican settlements in the area (Emory 1848: 23, 27). Yet, no bands of Indians were met between Bent's Fort and Santa Fe when General Kearney and his military force took New Mexico for the United States.

In 1850 George A. McCall (1851: 12) identified the territory of the New Mexican Utes as extending from the San Juan Mountains to the headwaters of the Arkansas, and he stated that they made forays only as far south as Abituin (Abiquiu), Taos, and Moratown (Mora). He estimated their population at four to five thousand and indicated that they did not have permanent villages or cultivated fields but subsisted chiefly on game.

CHAPTER SIX

THE COMANCHE

The Comanche were also Shoshonean speakers who apparently split about A.D. 1550 (Hale 1958: 107) from their closest linguistic relatives, the Shoshoni, living in Wyoming. The Comanche may have been living there also, before they first appeared on the northern frontier of New Mexico. This possibility is supported by Mooney (1896: 1043-1046) who stated that the Comanche speak virtually the same language as the Shoshonies of Wyoming where, within traditional memory, they had lived as neighbors. Thus, it is not surprising that sometimes in the historical literature the same name is applied to both. Often the names can be translated "Snake," as the Shoshoni were commonly called. The name Iatan, with many variations such as L'Iatan or Halitan, is most commonly applied to the Comanches, but it is sometimes also used for certain of their linguistic relatives. The Comanches, along with various other Shoshonean speakers, call themselves Numa whereas the name Comanche was applied to them by the Spanish. Mooney gives names applied to the Comanches by various tribes and the names used to designate sub-bands of the Comanche. Unfortunately, he equates the Padouca with Comanche, a common error that has been perpetuated. The Padouca were plains Apaches. This name was most commonly used to indicate the Kiowa Apaches.

The first mention of the Comanche in New Mexican documents was in 1706 when Juan de Ulibarri heard that Comanche, in league with Utes, planned to attack Taos pueblo (Thomas: 1935: 61). This attack did not materialize, but in 1716, again with the Utes, they raided Taos and some other Spanish settlements. The Spanish retaliated and attacked the Utes and Comanches where they were settled, near the Cerro de San Antonio, in the Rio Grande Valley, essentially at the present Colorado-New Mexico line. In 1694 the Spanish considered this area north of Taos as Ute territory (Espinosa 1942: 193) so it is likely that the 1706 date is close to the time that the Comanche arrived on the Central High Plains.

After this first appearance [1706] in New Mexican documents, the Comanches are mentioned frequently. During the early 1700s, especially between 1716 and 1730, they became a constant threat to Spanish, Pueblos and Apaches alike in northeastern New Mexico (Thomas 1935; D. Gunnerson 1974: 182-216). In 1719, Valverde led an expedition, described above, into southeastern Colorado to chastise Utes and Comanches who had recently forced Carlana Apaches to leave the area. Carlana Apaches served as guides for Valverde's party that saw the Comanches' trail,

but no Comanches. From the Arkansas River as far north as Limon, Colorado and from the foothills of the Rockies east to Las Animas the party sought Comanches in vain. While on the Arkansas River, Valverde met Cuartelejo Apaches who told him that their villages were being attacked by Utes, presumably allied with Comanches (Thomas 1935: 110-133; Gunnerson 1984). In 1727 the French wanted to make contact with the Comanches and enlisted the aid of Cuartelejo Apaches, who still lived in western Kansas, (Thomas 1935: 256) to do so. In 1723 Comanches attacked and killed many Jicarilla Apaches at La Jicarilla, just across the Sangre de Cristos east from Taos (Thomas 1935: 194). By about 1730 the Comanches so dominated the plains of western Kansas and eastern Colorado that they had forced the Cuartelejo Apaches out of the region, and by 1748 they had forced the Jicarilla Apaches to abandon their semipermanent villages east of the Sangre de Criscos, in New Mexico, although the Jicarilla continued to exploit the area from tipi camps (Gunnerson 1974: 224-226). In the early 1700s Apaches, though poorly armed, had formed something of a buffer between the Comanches and New Mexico, but by 1748 this barrier had ceased to be effective. Also, by the mid-1700s the Comanches became enemies of the Utes with whom they had been allied earlier. Since the Comanches functioned as a number of independent bands, friendships, trade, or animosities frequently did not apply equally to all of the Comanches. In 1739 Pierre and Paul Mallet, on their way to Santa Fe from Pawnee country in what is now eastern Nebraska, met Comanches on the Arkansas River well out from the mountains. On their return trip the Mallet brothers went east from Santa Fe and some ten days out again met Comanches, this time on the Canadian River, probably in the Texas panhandle (Thomas 1940: 15, 16; Folmer 1939).

Apparently by then, the Comanches had forced the Faraon Apaches to move west from their old territory on the Canadian. Thus, by about 1739 the Comanches were in control of most, if not all, of what is called the Central High Plains.

By the middle of the 1700s Comanches were being contacted directly by French traders. In 1748 a party of 33 Frenchmen were reported to be in El Quartelejo, in west central Kansas, formerly Apache country, trading with Comanches. The next year other Frenchmen, while traveling between Jumano country and Santa Fe, passed through Comanche territory, probably near the Arkansas River in southern Kansas or northern Oklahoma (Bolton 1914: I 58-59). In 1749 there were several Comanche villages on the Arkansas River, near the Rocky Mountains, visited by Frenchmen. The Comanches were accustomed to go into Taos to trade and several of the Frenchmen accompanied them (Bolton 1917). At least two of the French parties had left Wichita territory and followed the Arkansas to get to New Mexico. No other tribes were mentioned as being between the Jumanos (Wichitas) and the Comanches. During the middle 1700s the Comanches were well supplied with French guns and ammunition, primarily through Jumanos (Wichitas) and later in the century they were getting English arms. Between 1746 and 1748 the French had succeeded in making a treaty between the Comanches and the Jumanos (Wichitas) which suggests that the Comanches had expanded eastward (Thomas 1940: 17; Bolton 1917: 72). And, by 1751, the Comanches had established friendly relations with the Pawnee to the northeast (Thomas 1940: 20; Bolton 1917: 400).

In general, the Comanches served as a barrier to communication between European settlements in the lower Mississippi drainage and those in New Mexico (Bolton 1914, 1917). Spanish officials in Texas and Louisiana, in the mid-1700s, made repeated treaties with the Comanches, but the relationship continued to be basically one of hostility (Bolton 1914). Once the Comanches started getting French trade goods during the 1740s, they became increasingly hostile until about 1786. During this period, they committed numerous depredations, many of which have been gleaned from the literature by Kenner (1969: 36-52). In the 1750s Comanche raids on both Spanish and Pueblo settlements increased, although the Comanches still came arrogantly into Santa Fe and Taos to trade (Thomas: 1940). In 1751, 40 tipis of Comanches came to Taos while in the same year a party of over 300 Comanches attacked Pecos and Galisteo Pueblos. Governor Tomas Velez de Cachupin pursued the Comanches south from Galisteo and out onto the plains where the band divided. Some Comanches had their *rancherias* on the Rio Napestle (Arkansas) (Thomas 1940: 68-75). After their defeat by Cachupin in 1751, the Comanches were apparently less troublesome to New Mexico for a while, although in 1753 the Viceroy Conde de Revilla Gigedo stated that the Comanches, among others, continued their nightly raids although they were still coming into Santa Fe yearly to trade (Thomas: 1940: 111).

In 1767, after some 16 years of relative peace, the Comanches again became very hostile toward the Spanish, and remained so for twenty years (Thomas: 1940: 38-59, 165-213; Thomas 1932: 57-64). In 1768 Comanches, with their chief Green Horn, (Cuerno Verde) raided New Mexico from the north, hitting Ojo Caliente, Taos and Picuris. By 1772 they were said to be attacking New Mexico "from all directions" but

primarily from the north and east, raiding Pecos Pueblo, various other pueblos and settlements along the Rio Grande and even Albuquerque was attacked. Trade at Taos, however, continued. In 1774 one of many New Mexican expeditions against the Comanches attacked a *rancheria* 50 leagues (136 miles) east of Santa Fe. In the late 1770s Comanche raids continued, with the outlying eastern and northern Pueblos, from Taos to Pecos, being the most frequently raided, but Albuquerque and nearby settlements on the Rio Grande itself were not immune. In 1777 the Spaniards pursued one band of Comanches 100 leagues (273 miles) to the southeast, probably to near San Saba, Texas.

During the last half of the 1700s, the Comanches were an equally serious threat on the Texas frontier, frequently appearing as far southeast as San Antonio de Bexar. Raids were common on European settlements. The Lipan Indians had previously occupied part of the area but they were displaced by the Comanches who then essentially dominated the northwestern half of Texas (John 1975: 336-430, 531-556, 612-766). In 1770 Athanaze de Mezieres stated that the Comanche "are a people so numerous and so haughty that when asked their numbers, they make no difficulty of comparing it to that of the stars" and that they follow the buffalo north in the summer and south in the winter, raiding as far south as New and Old Mexico (Barry 1972: 29-30; Bolton 1914: 218). In 1785 Governor Esteban Rodriguez Miro, of Spanish Louisiana, states that the Laytanes (Comanches) inhabit the borders of New Mexico and dominate all of the neighboring tribes (Barry 1972: 33). Thomas (1932: 73), on the basis of his extensive research in the Spanish archives, summarized the location of the various Comanche bands as of 1775 as follows:

> "The Comanche at that moment constituted three well defined groups, Yupe, Yamparica and Cuchanec or Cuchantica. The Yupe occupied the region north of the Arkansas River as far as the southern part of present Wyoming; the Yamparica extended across the northern part of Colorado of today, and southward among the Yupe to the Arkansas; and between the Arkansas and the present Red River ranged the Cuchanec, Buffalo Eaters, whom Anza briefly described from information just furnished him by Francisco Xavier Ortiz, an emissary to these Comanche. Between the Pecos and the Red rivers, Ortiz found eight Cuchanec *rancherias* in a quadrangle roughly forty leagues square, that is, about one hundred miles square. Therein he estimated that the smallest *rancheria* had thirty tents, all eight, about seven hundred, and

that there were three to four warriors in each tent, i.e., between six and seven thousand souls. These Comanche, moreover, owned about nine hundred beasts of burden, including five herds of mares. More specifically he mentioned that Chief Canaquaipe ruled over one hundred and fifty-five tents, and Chief Ecueracapa, one hundred and fifty-seven. Eastward beyond these Cuchanec Ortiz reported others who ranged as far as the Jumano and Taovayas, then settled on lands in southern present Oklahoma and northern Texas."

When Juan Bantista de Anza, newly appointed governor, reached New Mexico in 1778, he learned that the Comanches were the scourge of the kingdom. He decided to go into their own country 200 Ute and Apache auxiliaries, northward along the west side of the Rio Grande, into the San Luis valley and then east across the mountains. Some 25 leagues (68 miles) north of the Arkansas River, near Castle Rock, Colorado, he attacked and thoroughly defeated a large group of Comanches. Their chief, Cuerno Verde ("Greenhorn"), with a small contingent of his band, was at the time attacking Taos Pueblo where he, too, was defeated. When de Anza, on his return south along the foothills, reached the Arkansas River he met up with Cuerno Verde and his small group on their way back from Taos to join the main part of the band. Anza attacked this war party and thoroughly defeated these Comanches near Rye, Colorado. Cuerno Verde, along with his son and heir apparent, as well as several other leaders, were all killed. An estimated 131 Comanches were slain. Perhaps because of the loss of the flamboyant Cuerno Verde, the next several years saw reduced hostility on the part of the Comanches. The Spanish continued to put pressure on the Comanches, both in Texas and New Mexico. In 1778 the Spanish learned that the Osage were giving the Comanches trouble in the east. In 1785 the Comanches came into New Mexico seeking peace. A council was held on the Arkansas River to discuss terms with de Anza, and in 1786 peace was formally made among the Spanish, Utes and Comanches. The Utes, however, resisted the idea of the Spanish establishing peace with the Comanches, then their arch enemies (Thomas 1932: 66-83).

Also, during the late 1700s and early 1800s, Pedro Vial, representing the government of New Mexico, made a number of efforts to establish and maintain peace between the Comanches and their more sedentary neighbors to the east (Loomis and Nasatir 1967; Barry 1972: 34-41). In 1787, during a peaceful period, the Yupes Comanches expressed a desire to settle down. The Spaniards built adobe houses for them at San Carlos, in the foothills of the mountains

near the Arkansas River (Thomas 1929). Half a year later the settlement was abandoned because of the death there of the wife of a chief. This did, however, mark the beginning of a period when Comanches were allied with New Mexicans against Apaches (Hackett 1934-46 III: 213; Kenner 1969: 53-77).

In 1788 Vial set out from Santa Fe to visit the Jumano (Wichita) villages and then went on to San Antonio de Bexar. The diary of Santiago Fernandez and four versions of the diary of Francisco Fragoso, both of whom accompanied him, have been translated by Loomis and Nasatir (1967: 316-368). Each of the diaries contains information not included in others, but in general they match and the route through Comanche territory can be reconstructed with reasonable certainty. On June 30, 1788, Vial reached the first Comanche village of 56 lodges, 3 leagues (8 miles) east of Tucumcari Mesa. This mesa still carries the name and has given its name to the nearby town in eastern New Mexico. On July 5 the party came to numerous Comanches and one of their villages near present Canyon, Texas, at the head of Palo Duro Canyon, through which flows the Prairie Dog Town Fork of the Red River, called then the Rio Blanco. The party continued to follow the Rio Blanco east, at times leaving the river by a few miles. On July 9, another Comanche village was discovered a few miles west of the Oklahoma-Texas line. Then on July 15, a very large settlement, having 372 dwellings according to Fernandez, was visited, probably near the mouth of the Pease River, some 44 miles west of Wichita Falls, Texas. On July 16 and 17 Fragoso reported additional Comanches, including a village of more than 200 lodges within the next 15 leagues (40 miles). The party would then have been at a point on the Red River essentially straight north of Wichita Falls and within less than 61 miles of the first Wichita village visited. This would indicate a very substantial Comanche population just to the south of what is known as the Central High Plains.

In 1806 Lt. Facundo Melgares, with a substantial military force, set out from Santa Fe and, after descending the "Red River" (probably the Canadian), met a large number of Comanches 233 leagues (355 miles) down the river (Jackson 1966 I: 324). Although the distance given is too great, the Comanches were probably in western Oklahoma. From here, Melgares struck northeast, crossed the Arkansas River and arrived at the Republican Pawnee village in southern Nebraska, near where the Republican River crosses the Kansas border. In 1808, Francisco Amangual led a Spanish party from San Antonio de Bexar [Texas] to Santa Fe in an attempt to establish a feasible wagon route between these two centers. On May 3, 1808, he met Yamparica Comanches before he had traveled half the distance. Although it is difficult to trace his route exactly, he was probably a little south of the Texas panhandle at the time. He continued to encounter Comanches until he was apparently into northeastern New Mexico. Here he met Spanish parties out hunting buffalo. This represents a switch from the earlier traders, Comancheros, who went out to trade with the Comanches for buffalo products, to Spanish hunters, Ciboleros, who procured their own meat and hides (Loomis and Nasatir 1967: 459-508).

During this first decade of the 1800s, the Comanches began to lose their dominance of the Central High Plains since tribes from the north such as the Arapaho, Cheyenne, Kiowa, Kiowa Apaches, Sioux, Crow and Shoshone, spread south to the Arkansas River and soon beyond. Groups from the east, especially various bands of the Pawnee and Wichita, continued, probably with increased frequency, incursions onto the high plains from their permanent villages closer to the Missouri River. Peace, such as it was, among Comanches, Utes, Navajos, and Spaniards in New Mexico lasted until about 1810. In the early 1800s the western movement of Americans disrupted the *status quo*. The revolt by Mexico, [1810] against Spain, diverted resources necessary for maintaining amicable relations with the Indians away from the northern frontier of New Mexico (Thomas 1932: 66-83).

The 1814 Lewis and Clark Map (Wheat 1954 II: Map 316) shows the Li-h-tan Band (Comanches) in the Rocky Mountains, extending south into the Rio del Norte (Rio Grande) drainage west of the headwaters of the Arkansas River. Several bands of Snakes (Shoshones) are shown in the mountains farther north. No Shoshonean speakers, however, are shown out on the plains, probably because the Comanche's main area was farther south, beyond the area with which Lewis and Clark were primarily concerned. Bell, of the Long expedition in 1820, met a small party of Comanches near the Great Bend of the Arkansas River in central Kansas. The party was returning from an aborted attack on the Osage (James 1823 II: 208). These Comanches were said to be "indistinguishable" from Kiowas, Kiowa Apaches and Arapahos. In 1821 Hugh Fowler, who was camped with a group of Kiowas on the Arkansas River, near the mouth of the Apishipa, described a rendezvous there. After three days, about 350 lodges of "Highatans" [Comanches] joined the Kiowas and the next day these were joined by "Arrapohos," "Kiowa Padduce" [Kiowa Apaches], "Cheans" [Cheyennes], and "Snakes" [Shoshones]." The Ietan [Comanches], however, were the most numerous (Coues 1970: 52-58).

In 1821, at the time Mexico gained its independence from Spain, Glenn James and John McKnight set out for Santa Fe, going up the Arkansas River, cutting south to the Cimarron River and then to the Canadian, which they followed west across the Texas panhandle, and toward its head. In the latter part of their journey the Comanches threatened the party and made it give up much of the merchandise that it was carrying. The party would probably have been massacred by Comanches some 8 or 10 days from Santa Fe, but it was saved by a friendly Comanche, Cordero, who brought a rescue party of [New] Mexican soldiers to its aid (Ghent 1936: 188-189).

In 1836 the Comanches were reported by Paul Ligueste Chouteau to: "Claim and occupy all the country bounded North by the Arkansas river, South by the Mexican Settlements, West by the Grand Cordillera, and East by the Cross Timbers. The numerical force of Comanches....is estimated....by the Mexican Government at 8,000 but, from my personal observations, I have been induced to calculate the number of Comanche warriors at 4,500." The Comanches allowed other tribes to live in their country: the Kiowas, their closest allies, the Cah-tah-kahs (Kiowa Apaches) who were with the Kiowas, and the Wichitas from whom the Comanches got corn (Barry 1972: 305; Foreman 1933: 148). In 1845 Lt. J. J. Abert (1846) set out from Bent's Fort on the Arkansas River, went up the Purgatory River, crossed Raton Mesa and followed down the Canadian River and "through the country of the camanche Indians." Abert (1846: 37-46) reported seeing a few Indians from about the time the party crossed the New Mexico-Texas border. About 31 miles farther east Comanches came into their camp on the Canadian. Still farther east, when the party was essentially north of Amarillo, Texas, it met another band of Comanches near whom were some Kiowas and several Crows. In the same general area, the Abert party saw a number of Spanish traders from New Mexico, called "Comancheros," with their Pueblo guides. Reportedly, they often came into this area to acquire horses and mules from the Indians. The Abert party continued east along the Canadian, and noted a few old camps which they attributed to Comanches, but they met no Indians in what is now western Oklahoma. In eastern Oklahoma they came to Creek and Quapaw villages (Abert 1856: 69). The map of the Abert/Peak expedition shows the territory of the "Comanchee and Kiowa Indians" being on both sides of the Canadian River for essentially the breadth of the Texas Panhandle (Abert 1846: map bound in back). Charles Bent (?) writing from Santa Fe in 1846 states: "East of the mountains of New Mexico, range the Commanches, a numerous and warlike people subsisting entirely by the Chase. Their different bands number in all about 2500 lodges or 12,000 souls. They have been at peace for many years with the New Mexicans but have carried on an incessant and destructive war with the Departments of Chihuahua,

Durango and Coahuila from which they have carried off and still hold as slaves, a large number of women and children, and immense herds of horses, mules and asses" (Abel 1915: 7).

Butler and Lewis (1846: 10-12), who went to the Comanches from New Orleans for the [U.S.] Indian Commission, stated that Comanches have an estimated total population of 14,300 and are subdivided into six distinct bands. Although the Comanches wander widely, the territory of each band is given as follows:

1. Yam-pa-ric-coes or "Root Diggers range generally on the headwaters of the Canadian and Red rivers."

2. Hoo-ish or "Honey Eaters inhabit the southern part of the Camanche country, bordering the settlements of Texas."

3. Co-che-ta-cahs or "Buffalo Eaters are located principally upon the headwaters of the Brazos."

4. Noo-nah or "people of the desert live upon the open plains or prairie, between the Colorado and Brazos rivers."

5. No-coo-nees or "people of the circle are located between the Colorado and Rio Grande."

6. Te-nay-wash or "people of the timber command the prairies and are the principle ones to be treated with and conciliated."

In 1850 George McCall (1851) reported that the Comanche visited eastern New Mexico at least once a year, but generally they wintered near the sources of the Brazos and Trinity Rivers of Texas. He further indicated that they met Mescelero Apaches on the Pecos River. Together they went to Chihuahua and Sonora returning to the Pecos with many mules and prisoners. Here they exchanged these with New Mexican traders for arms, ammunition, cloth, paint, etc. Some of the mules were eaten. The location of this trading rendezvous is not given, but from context it would be well below San Miguel, New Mexico. McCall gives the population of the Comanches as upwards of 12,000 souls.

In 1852 Captain Randolph B. Marcy (1853: 21-43) led an expedition up the Red River to the head of its North Branch (near Pampa, Texas). For several days before arriving, he had seen trails and camps, both recent and old, of large bands of Comanches, and probably Kiowas. He then worked his way south, exploring the other two branches of the Red River, and he noted additional Indian trails and camps; in one case some lodges had apparently been burned.

His descriptions are good and the place names that he gives are still in use, so one can follow his route with reasonable certainty. In 1853 a 280 lodge camp of Comanches was noted by John W. Gunnison's party on the Arkansas River near present Dodge City, [Kansas] the eastern edge of Comanche hunting territory, which they shared with the Kiowa. Just to the east was a narrow strip of "neutral ground." Beyond this, and extending east from about Larned, Kansas, was the hunting territory of the Osages, Kansas and Saks. A few miles west of the Comanche camp that, in turn, was a mile west of and across the river from Fort Atkinson, was a camp of Kiowas whose warriors had joined with the Cheyennes, Arapahos, Jicarilla Apaches and a few Comanches to attack the Pawnee (Beckwith 1855: 21). Further up the Arkansas, at the ruins of Bent's Old Fort (near Las Animas, Colorado), Beckwith (1855: 26) commented that it would be a good place for a military post "in the heart of Indian country, accessible to the resorts of the Comanches, Cheyennes, Arapahoes, Kioways, some bands of Apaches and even occasionally of the Utahs of New Mexico."

Captain Randolph Marcy led another expedition in 1855, this time to explore the Big Wichita River and the headwaters of the Brazos River (Marcy 1856). Of the Indians, he stated that the most populous tribe in Texas was the Comanches and that they were divided into three major groups. The Southern Comanches ranged primarily within Texas, between the Red and Colorado Rivers. The Middle Comanches, consisting of the "No-co-nies and Ten-na wees" bands, "spend their winters in Texas and in the summer move north across the Red river and the Canadian towards the Arkansas, in pursuit of the buffaloes." The Northern Comanches, whom Marcy considered much wilder than the others and responsible for most of the Comanche raids into Mexico, wintered on the Red River and wandered widely during the summer (Marcy 1856: 28-34). As part of John Pope's report of exploration, also in 1855, he described the Comanches as dominating the plains south of essentially the Arkansas River, from the 98th meridian, on the east, to the eastern base of the Llano Estacado and ranging as far south as Mexico. Accompanying them were small bands of other tribes, the largest and most powerful being the Kiowas. The Kiowas, however, were said to winter on the Arkansas, and its tributaries, in what is now southeast Colorado (Pope 1855: 22-24). Also in 1855, Colonel John Garland reported that the Comanches were being driven west from Texas and were hovering on the eastern border of New Mexico. Kenner (1969: 120-137) has noted a series of incidents relating to this change in the core area for the Comanches.

In 1856 Francis T. Bryan, who traveled east along the Republican River in southwestern Nebraska, stated that the Republican River bottom was a favorite hunting ground for the Cheyennes, Comanches, and Kiowas. His entry a few days earlier, when he was near the mouth of Frenchman Creek, stated that he was then in the very home of the Cheyennes who claimed the valley as their particular hunting territory (Bryan 1857: 473, 475). He apparently did not meet either Kiowas or Comanches here and the source of his information is not indicated. In 1867 a reservation was established in southwestern Oklahoma for the Comanche and by 1875 they, along with the Kiowa and Kiowa Apaches, were settled on it.

CHAPTER SEVEN

THE SHOSHONI

The Shoshoni provide the name for the Shoshonean linguistic family, which includes Utes and Comanches, the only others that got onto the plains, plus many bands in the Great Basin, the homeland of the more inclusive Uto-Aztecan family. In historic times, the Shoshoni occupied much of Wyoming and occasionally ventured into the Central High Plains to trade, raid and fight. The name "Snakes" or "Gens de Serpent" is commonly applied to the Shoshoni and less frequently to the Comanches. Presumably the Comanches split from the Shoshoni in about 1700 and moved from Wyoming onto southern Colorado.

In 1804, Lewis and Clark (1905 VI: 106-107) reported the Alitan or Snake Indians as living "in and about" the Rocky Mountains, roving from the Missouri River southward to the head of the Arkansas River, and having "immense quantities of horses, mules and asses;" sometimes trading with the Spanish in New Mexico. There appears to be some confusion between the Snakes (Shoshonis) and the Comanches, who were commonly called "Laitan." Perhaps the tribes are being lumped, since, according to Lewis and Clark, the nation is said to be divided into three tribes, the So-so-na, So-so'bu-bar, and I-a-kar, which in turn are divided into smaller, independent bands. Two of these bands were apparently also known as the West Aliatans and the La Playes. Of the West Aliatans, most probably Comanches, the statement is made that: "They have more intercourse with the Spaniards of New Mexico, than the Snake Indians."

Larocque, in his journal of 1805 (Hazlitt 1934: 19) noted that the Snakes traded with the Spanish, but their location was not indicated and it is not clear whether he was referring to the Shoshoni or the Comanches. John R. Bell (1957: 203), of Long's 1820 expedition, while on the Arkansas River in southeastern Colorado learned that the La Playes and So-so-nas, a band of the Snake Indians, had attached themselves to the great chief Bear's Tooth, but Bell did not actually see them. Bear's Tooth was an Arapaho, but he was also a recognized leader for the Kiowa, Kiowa Apaches, and, especially, the Cheyennes at that time. Near La Junta, Colorado, the Long party met Arapahos, Kiowas, Kiowa Apaches, a band of Cheyenne, a few Shoshoni and some Bald-heads (James 1823: II 60-61).

The Glenn-Fowler party of 1821 found Snakes (Shoshonis) with Comanches, Arapahos, Kiowas and Cheyennes in large camps on the Arkansas River near the site of Nepesta, Colorado (Ghent 1936: 190; Coues 1970: 58). In the 1830s Bent knew of Shoshonis visiting the Arkansas River region (Lavender 1954: 142, 161, 182).

CHAPTER EIGHT

THE ARAPAHO

Very little is known about the Arapaho before the early 1800s. Previous history, based to a large extent on tradition, has been summarized by Virginia Trenholm (1970: 3-32). These Algonquian speakers once lived in Minnesota and migrated west to the Missouri River in the 1700s. One of the early names for the Arapaho was the Bison-path people, a name by which they were known to the Minnetarees (James 1823 II: 199). The French translation of this name, Gens de Vache ("People of the buffalo"), was also commonly used, as were "Big Bead" and "Blue Bead" People. Apparently the names Gros Ventre of the Prairie, Staetan, Kites, Castahana and Water-fall People were also applied to the Arapaho, but were less commonly used. There is confusion on some of these names because, for example, the Hidatsa were commonly called Gros Ventre and the Crows were also called Kites. *Gens de Vache* was corrupted into numerous forms such as Kanenavish, Kannenawish and Canninabich. Lewis and Clark (1804 I: 190), however, in a list of tribes of the Upper Missouri includes the following Synonmy, Kun-na-nar-Wesh — (Gens des vach) "Blue Beads." Although they do not discuss it, they apparently recognized the "Kun-na-nar-Wesh" was simply a corruption of the French name "Gens de vache." There has also been speculation as to the origin and meaning of the modern name "Arapaho", under which they have been most commonly known for over a century and a half. Trenholm (1970: 32) suggests that the name Arapaho may be derived from either a Siouan word meaning "lots of Tattoes" or a Pawnee word meaning "trader." Dunbar (cited in Hodge 1907-1910 I: 72) suggested that the name for the Arapaho was from the Pawnee word "tirapihu" or "laralpihu" meaning trader. Lewis and Clark (1905 VI: 87) gave 'Ar-hah-pa-hoo' as the pronunciation of the name by which the Republican band of the Pawnees called themselves.

A more probable origin of the name Arapaho has been proposed by D. Gunnerson (1983). She notes that the name was used in 1812 by Manuel Lisa, a Spanish speaking native of New Orleans who operated trading establishments on the Upper Missouri. In Spanish the word means "tattered and dirty clothing" which is also the meaning of the Kiowa name for the Arapaho. Perhaps it was Lisa himself who translated the Kiowa name into Spanish and applied it initially to this tribe. In 1811, a party including Lisa, Bradbury, and Brackenridge, traveled up the Missouri River together. Lisa stayed at his post on the Missouri, while Bradbury returned to St. Louis that same year, and Brackenridge continued on to the Pacific northwest returning east the next year. Each contributes to our information on the Arapaho.

In 1811, Lisa sent 23 hunters to trade specifically with the Arapahos who then lived on the headwaters of the Platte and perhaps also on the headwaters of the Arkansas. This is stated in a letter written by Lisa to officials in New Mexico and carried there by Don Carl Sanguinet (Bolton 1913). Lisa also said that Arapahos had told some of his men that Spanish traders visited them every year. Lisa's real goal was to trade directly with the Spaniards, and it was to them the letter was addressed. In Bradbury's account of his trip up the Missouri with Lisa and Brackenridge in 1811 (not 1810 as reported by Trenholm (1970: 32), he described a highly decorated robe possessed by a Cheyenne, and learned that it "had been purchased from the Arapahoes, or Big Bead Indians, a remote tribe, who frequent the Rocky Mountains." The Cheyenne was one of a small group of visitors in an Arikara village.

Brackenridge (1814: 85) located the Kan-ne-na-wish on the heads of the Yellowstone River and estimated their population as 5,000 souls. It is not clear where Brackenridge got this information, which is presented in a table. There is no indication in the journal that he had any first hand information and he does not include the Kannenawish or Arapaho in his tribal descriptions in the text. However, there was published as an Appendix by Brackenridge (1917: 297-302), an account by Robert Steuart, who was with the party that continued to the Columbia River. The account was published previously in the *Missouri Gazette*, on June 28, 1812. Steuart reported that when the party that he was with had ascended the Columbia 600 miles, it met a Joseph Miller who had been among "the nations called Blackarms and Arapahays" considerably to the south and east. This newspaper account, published in 1812, may be the first use of the name Arapaho in print, but Manuel Lisa seems to have known about it earlier.

It is still not clear whether the Spanish in New Mexico knew the Arapaho by that or some other name, even though Spaniards went out to trade with them. There has been speculation that the Arapahos may have been known in New Mexico as Cuampas, but D. Gunnerson (1983) has convincingly demonstrated that the Cuampas were the Kiowas or a band of Kiowas. It seems highly likely that the Arapahos were among the tribes called by New Mexicans "Nations of the North," in the early 1800s. These included such other tribes as the Cheyennes, Kiowas, Kiowa Apaches and Blackfeet. The Spaniards of Texas also referred to "Nations of the North," but they meant tribes of northeastern Texas, Oklahoma, Kansas and Nebraska who, for the most part, were sedentary Caddoan speakers (Bolton 1914).

The information on the Arapaho provided by Lewis and Clark (1905: 80-113; Jefferson 1806: 37) is somewhat confusing. They use two spellings, Kanenavish and Canenavich, and give as synonyms: Staetan, Cas-ta-ha-na, Gens de Vache and Blue Beads. They also give as a nickname "Kites" which is more commonly applied to the Crow. The Arapaho territory was said to be on the headwaters of the Bighorn and Loup Rivers. On the Clark map, copied by King in 1805 and in 1806 (Tucker 1942: Plate XXXI; Moulton 1983: Map 32a, 32b) are several of the names: Canenavick, Staetan, Castanaha, and Kanenavech placed just south of the Black Hills where the Cheyenne, White and Quick (Niobrara) Rivers head and at the head of the north fork of the Platte. On the 1814 Lewis and Clark map (Wheat 1954 II: Map 316), the Kanenavish are shown on both sides of the Platte River at the forks, the cas-ta-ha-na at the head of the south branch of the Platte; the "Staetan or Kites" are at the head of the White River. The Lewis and Clark (King) 1805 map (Wheat 1954: Map 248) shows the Kanenavich halfway between the mouth and the head of the Padouca (north) fork of the Platte and the Castahana at its head; the Staetan are between the heads of the North Platte and the Quicurre (Niobrara) Rivers. These multiple names may represent different bands of the Arapaho.

In 1812-1813 Ezekiel Williams wintered with a camp of Arapahos on the headwaters of the Arkansas River and returned to them in 1814, with Joseph Philbert (Weber 1971: 42; Barry 1972: 70-72). Williams found the Arapaho very friendly toward the Europeans. In 1815 Auguste P. Chouteau and Jules de Mun received a trading license and went to Arapaho country, on the Arkansas headwaters (Barry 1972: 74). Stephen Long's party, in 1820, learned that about 1816 there had been a large group of Indians gathered on Grand-camp Creek, a tributary of the South Platte River. "On that occasion three nations of Indians, namely, the Kiawas, Arrapahoes, and Kaskaias or Bad-hearts [Kiowa Apaches], had been assembled together, with forty-five French hunters in the employ of Mr. Choteau and Mr. Dumun of St. Louis. They had assembled for the purpose of holding a trading council with a band of Shiennes. These last had been recently supplied with goods by the British traders on the Missouri, and had come to exchange them with the former for horses. The Kiowas, Arrapahoes, etc., who wander in the extensive plains of the Arkansas and Red river, have always had great numbers of horses....The

British traders annually supply the Minnetarees [Hidatsa] or Gros Ventres of the Missouri with goods; from these they pass to the Shiennes and Crow Indians, who, in turn, barter them with remoter tribes" (James 1823 I: 502-503).

No Indians were encountered by the Long party from the time it left the Pawnee [tribes] in eastern Nebraska until it reached the Arkansas River near the Rocky Mountains in southern Colorado. On the Arkansas River, not far from La Junta, Colorado, the Long party met Arapaho, Kiowa, Kiowa Apache, a band of Cheyenne, a few Shoshones and some Bald-heads, tribes that normally dominated eastern Colorado and western Kansas. These tribes were returning from fighting the Spanish on the Red River (James 1823 II: 60-61). The party was puzzled by the fact that: "The people called Padoucas have been represented as residing in the district now under consideration, but are not to be found unless this name is synonymous with that of [one]....of the six nations already enumerated" (James 1823 II: 64-65).

It is clear from the account of Bell's party of Long's expedition of 1820 (Bell 1957: 191-202; James 1823 II: 176-184) as it moved down the Arkansas River near Las Animas, Colorado, that the Arapahos, under their head chief, Bear's Tooth, were the dominant Indians of this area. On the 26th of July, 1820, four chiefs presented themselves in Bell's camp as representatives of the four "different nations here associated together, and consisting of the Kiaways, Kaskaias, or Bad-hearts [Kiowa Apaches], Sheiennes (sometimes written Chayenne), and Arrapahoes" (James 1823 II: 176). Bell (1957: 191) refers to the same tribes but with slightly different spellings: Kiawas, Chayenne, Kaskaya and Aerapaho. Later, in the same description of this encampment, one finds the statement: "The Bear-tooth is the grand chief of the Arrapahoes, and his influence extends over all of the tribes of the country in which he roves. He is said to be very favorably disposed towards white people, and to have afforded protection, and a home in his own lodge, to a poor and miserable American, who had had the good fortune to escape from the barbarity and mistaken policy of the Mexican Spaniards, and from the horrors of a Spanish prison" (James 1823 II: 184).

Of all the tribes that lived on the plains and in the foothills of eastern Colorado in the early 1800s, the Arapaho were apparently the most friendly to Europeans. In 1821 Jacob Fowler wintered with them and found them civil to European habits and, while he was living near the Arapahos in 1822, they actually encircled his lodge with 250 tipis to protect his party from a Comanche attack (Trenholm 1970: 42-45).

In 1835 Colonel Henry Dodge explored westward up the Platte and the South Platte rivers to the Rocky Mountains, then south along the foothills. He commented that: "The valley of the Fontaine que Bouille [Manitou Springs] is very much frequented by the Indians, especially by the Arepahas, who come up here in the fall to gather wild fruit that grows in abundance near the mountains" (Dodge 1836: 22-23). He also reported that the Arapaho frequently pitched their lodges and lived for a considerable length of time in the summer on the pass leading from the plains to Manitou Springs (Dodge 1836: 22). Earlier, when he was somewhere near the northeastern corner of Colorado, he stated that: "This section of country is what is called the neutral ground, and extends from the forks of the Platte [at North Platte, Nebraska] almost to the foot of the mountains. It will not admit of the permanent residence of any Indians, and is only frequented by the war parties of different nations.

The Arepahas and the Cheyenes sometimes move into this country for a short time during the summer, to hunt buffalos" (Dodge 1836: 19). It was not until Dodge (1836: 23) was camped on the Arkansas near the mouth of Fountain Creek that he found Arapahos, whom he was seeking. Fifty lodges of Arapahos were camped along the south side of the Arkansas, and the rest of the tribe, with a large number of Cheyennes, were hunting buffalo two days away, between the Arkansas and Platte Rivers.

In 1842 John C. Fremont found an Arapaho hunting camp on the South Platte River, near present day Fort Morgan, Colorado. Camping a little apart from about 105 lodges of Arapahos were 20 lodges of Cheyennes (Fremont 1845: 173). Also in 1842, Rufus Sage (1956: 54-55) met some Arapahos in the Denver area to whom he attributed the territory between the Arkansas and South Platte Rivers. Shortly before, he had met some Cheyennes a little farther north near the South Platte River. A map included in the report of the Abert-Peck expedition shows the territory of the Arapaho and Cheyenne Indians as occupying Colorado east of the Rocky Mountains, between the South Platte and the Arkansas Rivers (Abert 1846). Charles Bent, writing from Santa Fe in 1846, made the following statement: "The Cheyennes and Arrapahoes range through the country of the Arkansas and its tributaries on the north of this Department [New Mexico]. They live almost entirely on the Buffalo, and carry on a considerable trade, both with the Mexicans and the Americans, in Buffalo robes, for which they obtain all the necessaries not derived from the Buffalo. They are a roving people and have for many years been on friendly terms with the New Mexicans. The Arrappahoes number about 400 lodges, 2000 souls. The Cheyennes 300 lodges, 1500 souls" (Abel 1915: 7).

In 1842 Sage (1956: 67-68), while traveling south along the foothills, encountered a band of Arapahos near present Denver. He gives their territory as extending from the South Platte to the Arkansas River with an extent of about 45,000 square miles. Some 62 miles farther north he met some Cheyennes "who," he said "at this time occupy a portion of the Arapaho lands, bordering on the South Fork [of the Platte River] and its affluents" (Sage 1956: 54-55). According to Sage the Arapaho had some 252 lodges and were friendly to all their neighbors, especially Europeans, except for the Pawnee and Utahs. They met regularly to trade with the "Sioux, Cheyennes, Cumanches, and Kuyawas." Some 15 lodges of Blackfeet were among the Arapahos. The boiling springs just west of Colorado Springs, Sage noted, were called the Medicine Fountain by the Arapaho who venerated the area and often bestowed gifts here (Sage 1956: 75). In 1843 Sage (1956 II: 253-256, 265) reported a band of Arapahos well up a branch of the South Platte River near Brush, Colorado. The Arapahos at first had mistaken the Sage party for Pawnees, their enemies, whom they would have attacked. About 19 miles away was a camp of six or seven hundred lodges of Arapahos, Cheyennes, and Sioux. Sage provides an account of the colorful and exuberant group as it broke camp and moved out. The area just to the east of the headwaters of the Republican River, Sage (1956 II: 262) "considered very dangerous — it being the war-ground of the Pawnees, Caws [Kansa], Chyennes, Sioux, and Arapahoes." The next year (1844) Sage (1956 II: 295) passed a village of Arapahos on the Arkansas River near where the Santa Fe Trail crossed it in southwestern Kansas.

In 1850 George A. McCall (1851: 12) stated that the Cheyennes and Arapahos adjoined the Utes, who were to the west, and ranged from the headwaters of the Arkansas eastward onto the plains. They were characterized as subsisting entirely on the buffalo, and being friendly toward Europeans. Together they numbered about 3,500 souls. In 1856 while on an exploring expedition in and near the foothills of the Rockies in northeastern Colorado, Francis Bryan (1857: 467) encountered a camp of Arapahos under chief Little Owl. They were on one of the small northern tributaries of the Cache la Poudre, probably north of Fort Collins, near the Wyoming line. On an 1867 map by General Warren, Arapaho territory is shown as southeastern Colorado and southwestern Kansas.

By the middle 1800s the Arapaho were apparently a less formidable power on the high plains than were the Cheyenne with whom the Arapaho continued to be allied. These two tribes, along with others, particularly the Kiowa and Kiowa Apaches, continued to roam widely across the Central High Plains, hunting and fighting. Much of this later history of the Arapaho has been summarized by Trenholm (1970). Their frequent encounters with the U.S. military, both friendly and hostile, have been well documented in numerous letters and reports prepared by the U.S. Congress and the War Department, which at that time included Indian Affairs.

CHAPTER NINE
THE CHEYENNE

The Cheyennes, who along with their Algonquian speaking relatives the Arapaho, dominated much of the Central High Plains during the mid-1800s, also had their origin in western Minnesota. They probably moved to south-central South Dakota in the 1700s and by the very early 1800s parts of these two tribes roamed over much of eastern Colorado, pushing the Comanches south. It is not clear, however, whether there was a close friendship between the Arapaho and the Cheyenne before the southern divisions of both tribes moved onto the high plains. The Arapaho, who apparently arrived there first and were soon joined by the Cheyenne, were initially the dominant tribe. In 1820 the Arapaho chief Bear's Tooth, was the recognized leader of several loosely-allied tribes including the southern Cheyenne. By the mid-1800s, however, the Cheyennes were stronger and the Arapahos received less notice. The southern bands of these two tribes functioned together so much that one rarely finds accounts of one in which the other is not also mentioned. Each tribe tended to specialize—the Arapaho in hunting, the Cheyenne in trading. The history of the Cheyenne, especially the Southern Cheyenne, after the 1830s, is well presented by Berthrong (1963: 76 ff) and Grinnell (1956). Much of the history they cover centers around the various military engagements that the Cheyenne had with U.S. Government troops, especially after the mid-1800s.

Much of what we know about the earlier history of the Cheyenne was recorded by Lewis and Clark (Allen 1814 I: 94-95, 109) who learned that they "Were once a numerous people and lived on the Chayenne, a branch of the Red River of Lake Winniped." They had been forced west by the Sioux and settled in a fortified village on the "southern side of the Missouri below the Warreconne." Sioux pressure again forced them to take up a nomadic life at the head of the Cheyenne River from where they occasionally visit the Arikaras. In 1804 the Cheyenne were said to number 300 men. From a French trader named Valle, who had passed the previous winter with the Cheyenne, Lewis and Clark learned that "they steal horses from the Spanish settlements, a plundering excursion which they perform in a month's time." They [the Cheyenne] also give the name "Sharha" for the Cheyennes. Lewis and Clark (1905 VI: 100) reported that the Cheyennes or Chien (Dog) then lived on the Chien (Cheyenne) River and roved on both sides of the Black Hills. At this time, they no longer cultivated the soil as they formerly had when they lived "on the Cheyene River a fork of the Red River of Lake Winipique." On the 1814 Lewis and Clark Map (Wheat 1954 II: Map 316)

one finds the "Chayenns or Sharha" in what is obviously the Black Hills, near the headwaters of both branches of the Cheyenne River. The information on the map is said to be copied from the original drawing of William Clark. It is interesting that in 1804-1806, the Kanenavish (Arapaho) are shown well south of the Cheyennes which fits, as discussed elsewhere, with the arrival of these two tribes, in that order, on the Arkansas.

When Larocque was among the Mandan in central North Dakota during 1805, neighboring tribes were listed as the Assiniboines, Sioux, Ricaras and Cheyennes (Hazlitt 1934: 6). The implication was that the Cheyennes lived west and/or south of the Mandan. The earliest reference suggesting that the Cheyennes lived on the Central High Plains apparently dates from 1806. In the summer of that year Pedro Vial and two Cuampe (Kiowa?) chiefs brought James Purcell ("Pursley") and two Frenchmen into Santa Fe. While there, the Cuampa chiefs indicated that they had just recently established themselves on the headwaters of the Platte and Arkansas Rivers, about 40 leagues (112 miles) from Taos and asked for peace and permission to trade with the Spanish for both themselves and their allies the Sayenas (Cheyennes) and Aas (Crows?). By implication, these allies were living either with or near the Cuampas.

In 1811 John Bradbury (1817: 124) met several Cheyennes in an Arikara village where they were visiting. Of the Cheyenne he said, "This nation has no place of residence, but resorts chiefly about the Black Hills, near the head of the Chayenne river, having been driven from their former place of residence, near the Red River of Lake Winnipie, by the Sioux. Their number is now inconsiderable, as they scarcely muster 100 warriors." In 1820 the portion of the Long party under John R. Bell met Cheyennes, allied with Kiowas, Kiowa Apaches, and Arapahos, along the Arkansas River in southeastern Colorado (Bell 1957: 191 ff; James 1823 II: 176 ff). Bell learned that:

> "The Shiennes or Shawhays, who have united their destiny with these [Arapaho] wanderers, are a band of seceders from their own nation, and some time since on the occurrence of a serious dispute with their kindred on Shienne river of the Missouri, flew their country, and placed themselves under the protection of the Bear-tooth [head chief of the Arapahos].

"These nations have been for the three past years [before 1820], wandering on the head waters and tributaries of Red river [in Texas], having returned to the Arkansas, only the day which preceded our first interview with them, on their way to the mountains, at the sources of the Platte River. They have no permanent town, but constantly rove, as necessity urges them, in pursuit of the herds of bisons, in the vicinity of the sources of the Platte, Arkansa, and Red rivers" (James 1823 II: 186-187).

This statement could be interpreted as dating the split between the northern Cheyenne and the southern Cheyenne from 1817, but as will be discussed later, this might not be the case. A little farther down the Arkansas, a "Shienne" war party, returning from an attack on Pawnee Loups [Skidi], was encountered by the Bell party (James 1823 II: 197). Bell noted that the Cheyenne were habitually at war with all of the nations of the Missouri. He also found Cheyennes camped with Arapahos near Lamar, Colorado, on the Arkansas River. In this particular instance, these tribes had, shortly before, acted in concert with Kiowas and Kaskaia [Kiowa Apaches] in attacking some Spaniards on the Red River (James 1823 II: 176, 60, 187).

In 1821 Jacob Fowler identified the "Cheans" (Cheyennes) along with Comanche, Arapahos, Kiowa Apaches, Kiowas, and Shoshonis at a large rendezvous on the Arkansas River near the mouth of the Apishapa River in southeastern Colorado. A few days later, Fowler learned that the Arapahos had traded with the Cheyennes of the Missouri the previous summer (Coues 1970: 58, 64). This would suggest sporadic visiting of the Arkansas River region by the Cheyennes by 1820. Thomas Fitzpatrick, writing in 1847, said that the "Arapohoes" occupied the Arkansas River area long before the Cheyennes had seen it and that twenty years before, that is in 1827, the Arapahos were in possession of land from the Arkansas to north of the South Platte River while the Cheyennes lived between the Black Hills and the Missouri River (Trenholm 1970: 48).

Henry Atkinson (1825: 10) stated that the Cheyennes were "driven by the Sioux some years since, from the Red river country across the Missouri, and now inhabit the country on the Chyenne River, from its mouth, back to the Black Hills." He estimated a population of 3000, of which 550 to 600 were warriors. "Their principal rendezvous is toward the Black Hills, and their trading ground at the mouth of the Cherry river, a branch of the Chayenne, 40 miles above its mouth." It is not clear whether these were northern Cheyennes who had remained in the Black Hills area or whether also included were southern Cheyennes who had

gone back from the Arkansas River or whether the Cheyenne had not yet split into two bands. In 1835, while among cheyenns at Bent's Old Fort on the Arkansas, Henry Dodge (1835: 23-25) noted that the Cheyennes had formerly lived on the Missouri River where General Atkinson had visited them in 1825, and that shortly thereafter they moved south and joined the Arapahos.

In 1835 Dodge (1835: 23-25) found two villages of Cheyennes camped along the Arkansas River, above "Messrs, Bent, and St. Vrain's trading establishment" (Bent's Old Fort near Las Animas, Colorado). The Cheyennes were "going out against the Comanches." Earlier, Dodge learned that a large number of Cheyennes were hunting buffalo with the main body of the Arapahos between the Platte and Arkansas Rivers, about two days out from the confluence of Fountain Creek and the Arkansas. At Bent's Old Fort, Dodge met a few Blackfeet that were living with the Cheyennes. It was learned that the Cheyennes had recently made peace with the Osage, but that they were at war with the Comanches, Kiowas, Pawnees, and Arikaras. Dodge was instrumental in establishing peace between the Cheyennes and the Pawnee and Arikaras. He estimated the Cheyenne population to be 200 to 220 lodges, 660 men, for a total of 2640 souls. While at Bent's Old Fort, Dodge held a council with chiefs and warriors of the Cheyennes, Arapahos, Gros-ventres, and Blackfeet present. About 50 miles down the Arkansas from Bent's Old Fort, nearly to the modern Colorado-Kansas line, Dodge met another band of Cheyennes, one that was not at the recent council. The next day a party of Skidi Pawnee and Arikara arrived to make peace with the Cheyennes. This called for another council. Dodge noted that at one time the Arikara had lived with the Cheyennes. From there on to Fort Leavenworth, Dodge did not mention meeting any Indians.

Rufus Sage, in 1842 (1956: 54-55), met some Cheyennes near the South Platte River, some 62 miles north of Denver, where they occupied a portion of Arapaho lands. He stated, "Some six or eight years since, they inhabited the country in the vicinity of the Cheyenne and White Rivers and the North Fork of the Platte, from whence they were driven by hostile incursions of the Sioux, who now hold in quiet possession the whole of that territory" (Sage 1956: 67-68). Again, it is not clear whether northern or southern Cheyennes were involved. It is conceivable that the formal split between the two bands did not take place until about 1840, and that the Cheyennes previously noted south of the Platte River represented groups that came briefly into this region from their home territory in the Black Hills area.

In 1842 and 1843 Cheyenne and Arapaho were reported on the South Platte River, near the mountains, by John

C. Fremont (1845: 18, 23, 28-30, 111) who, in 1844, reported them with Sioux, Kiowas, and Comanches on the Arkansas River, about 20 miles below Bent's Old Fort in southeastern Colorado. The map included in the report of the Abert-Peck expedition from Bent's Old Fort south to, and then east along, the Canadian River shows the territory of the "Arapahoes and Cheyenn Indians" as essentially all of Colorado east of the Rockies between the South Platte and the Arkansas Rivers (Abert 1846).

In the fall of 1847, Fitzpatrick was at Bent's Old Fort where he met with Cheyennes and "Aripohoes" who for the most part were then enemies of the Comanches. He reported that "The Cheyennes claim this river [Arkansas] and the surrounding country, without any definite or defined limits; and, together with the Aripohoes and Sious, occupy indiscriminately the whole country along the eastern base of the Rocky mountains, from the northern frontier of New Mexico up to the Missouri River, without regard to lines of limitations of boundry" (Fitzpatrick 1848: 243). He gave the population of the Cheyennes as 280 lodges and not more than 500 warriors and of the Arapahoes as 350 lodges with 800 warriors. In 1850 G. A. McCall (1851: 12) stated that the Cheyennes and Arapahos ranged from the headwaters of the Arkansas River eastward onto the plains, that they subsisted entirely on the buffalo, were friendly toward Europeans and together numbered about 3,500.

In its findings, the U.S. Indian Claims Commission (1974: 3, 66-67) stated that, according to the Fort Laramie Treaty of 1851, the "territory of the Cheyennes and Arrapahoes" extended from the North Platte River south to the Arkansas River and from the main range of the Rocky Mountains east to a line roughly midway between the 100th and 101st meridians. This would include the eastern third of Colorado, the western quarter of Kansas, and smaller sections of southwestern Nebraska and southeast Wyoming. Essentially the northern four-fifths of what is called the Central High Plains is included. Cheyenne and Arapaho treaties, reservations, and late history are summarized by Ekirich (1974).

In 1856 while F.T. Bryan (1857: 471) was exploring east along the North Branch of the Republican River, which he called Rock Creek, he came upon a large camp of Cheyennes. The camp was 8 miles upstream from where Rock Creek (North Fork of the Republican) joins with the Arickare Branch, or about 7 miles west of the Colorado-Nebraska line. Some of the Cheyennes he met had recently been attacked by Captain Stuart. Farther down the Republican River, shortly before Bryan (1857: 473) reached the mouth of Frenchman Creek (which still bears that name) he noted that his party was "in the very home of the Cheyennes, who claim this valley as their particular hunting ground." When he was some 68 miles farther down the Republican River, Bryan (1857: 475) commented that: "The bottoms on this river afford subsistence to immense herds of buffaloes and elks. The Cheyennes, Comanches, and Kiowas make it their favorite hunting ground." The implication was that a substantial part of the Republican valley in southwestern Nebraska was included. The source of his information is not given and there is no indication that he met either Comanches or Kiowas here; he had, however, met a large band of Cheyennes up river, to the west.

G. K. Warren (1858: 667-668), whose main concern was with tribes in Nebraska and the Dakotas, gave the location of the "Sheyennes" as between the Platte and Arkansas Rivers. Warren reported that, in 1857, to escape from Colonel Sumner's expedition, some Cheyennes took refuge with the Dakotas in the neighborhood of the Black Hills. An estimated 300 to 500 Cheyennes (probably an exaggeration) were killed during the Sand Creek Massacre which took place in November 1864 at the bend of the Big Sandy Creek, about 40 miles north of Fort Lyon, Colorado. Much of a large winter camp was destroyed by a group of volunteers under the command of J.M. Chivington. A few Arapahos were among the Cheyennes. This military action was uncalled for and received a great deal of adverse reaction from the public. The documents relating to this incident fill several volumes (Carroll 1973). Trenholm (1970) provides a summary of the Sand Creek Massacre.

Following the Sand Creek massacre, the Indian War of 1865 ensued involving all of the plains tribes from the Red River of the north to the Red River of the south. The Indians again were willing to agree to peace, but in April 1867 General Handcock with a force of 1400 men burned down, without any particular provocation, a camp of 300 lodges of Cheyennes along with those of some of Arapahos and friendly Sioux. This action against the Cheyenne was, incidentally, the first Indian engagement in which General George A. Custer was involved. These southern Cheyennes and Arapahoes were within the hunting territory that had been assigned to them by the Treaty of October 1851 (Leavenworth; Wynkoop; Sanborn; Taylor; all in Otto et al 1867: 84-96, 111-112). The site of the Handcock attack, located 32 miles west of Fort Larned, Kansas, has been investigated archeologically (Miller 1977: 82; Millbrook 1973). Such attacks of the U.S. Military on the Cheyennes and Arapahos probably did much to trigger the hostilities of the next few years.

A series of documents concerning Indian hostilities on the southern plains was compiled in early winter of 1868 for the U.S. Senate by the Secretary of War (Scofield *et al* 1869). General William T. Sherman recognized that General Phil Sheridan, at Fort Hays, Kansas, was engaged in open warfare with Cheyennes, Arapahoes, Comanches, Kiowas, and Apaches, but other military leaders hoped to maintain peace. The Indians involved were mainly south of the Arkansas River, near Old Fort Cobb in western Oklahoma. The Cheyennes, under chief Black Kettle, were the most influential (Schofield *et al* 1869: 4, 6-26). Considerable difficulty was encountered in trying to keep the natives on their reservations, apparently due in large part to the U.S. Government's not providing supplies on time. Black Kettle wanted peace and on November 20, 1868, reported that his camp of 180 lodges was on the Washita River, 40 miles east of Antelope Hills (in Oklahoma, on the Texas line) (Schofield *et al* 1869: 22). One week later, early on the morning of November 27, 1868, Lieutenant Colonel (Brevet Major General) G.A. Custer, commanding 11 troops of the 7th cavalry, attacked Black Kettle's camp by surprise. The entire camp was destroyed. Some 103 warriors, including Black Kettle, were reported killed, and large quantities of supplies were captured. Fighting continued most of the day as fleeing Indians were pursued (Custer *in* Schofield *et al* 1869: 27-29). In addition to Black Kettle's band, Kiowas under Satanta, and Arapahos under Little Raven were camped near by and they joined with the Cheyennes in the fight. In reports by various U.S. Military Officers, prepared a few days after the "Battle of the Washita River," there was a general impression that many of the natives were not hostile to the U.S. Government. By late winter the purpose of the campaign, to force plains Indians onto reservations that had been established for them, was essentially accomplished. This did not terminate military conflict with the Southern Cheyenne, but the intensity decreased in the southern and central plains. A description of the "Battle of the Washita" is described by Lawrence Frost (1960) in *Great Western Indian Fights*.

In June 1869 General (then Colonel) Carr set out up the Republican River to clear the valley of Indians. In July he attacked the elite Cheyenne Dog Soldiers led by Tall Bull. A decisive battle took place at Summit Springs, not far south of the South Platte River near the site of today's Fort Morgan, Colorado (King 1963: 94-119). King considers "Summit Springs to be the last significant Indian battle on the central plains." Southern Cheyenne were joined by Northern Cheyenne in Indian Territory (Oklahoma) during 1878. Some of the Northern Cheyenne, under Dull Knife and other chiefs, "escaped" from Fort Reno. They started north across western Kansas and Nebraska but were captured by the U.S. military and taken to Fort Robinson Nebraska (Sheridan 1882: 94-98).

The later history of the Cheyenne and Arapaho has been summarized by Gussow (1974), Hafen (1974), Ekirch (1974) among others, and in the findings of the Indian Claims Commission (1974). George B. Grinell (1915) authored a classic study of the Cheyenne.

CHAPTER TEN

THE BLACKFEET

The Blackfeet, also an Algonkian-speaking tribe, lived in the northern plains, but some of them did get to the Central High Plains from time-to-time. In fact, parties of Blackfeet even went south into Mexico, following the Old North Trail which hugged the eastern foothills of the Rockies (McClintock 1910). In 1813, Arapahos told Manuel Lisa's employee Charles Sanguinet that Blackfeet had killed the trapper Champlain and two companions of Ezekiel Williams, presumably on the upper Arkansas River in Colorado. Snakes (Shoshoni), however, said that it had been Arapahos who did the killing (Weber 1971: 42). In any case, the Blackfeet were then known to the tribes along Arkansas.

Although Henry Atkinson (1825: 11-12) did not contact the Blackfeet, he learned that they inhabited the area between the Falls of the Missouri River [Great Falls] and the Rocky Mountains. They made war excursions to the south as far as the Big Horn. Their hunting territory embraced the three forks of the Missouri. Alphonso Wetmore (1832) described his experiences, along the Santa Fe Trail, of a decade earlier. In addition to "Panis, Chians, Comanches, Kiowas, and Arapahoe Indians," he reported that in 1821 "The Blackfeet Indians have this year, for the first time, made their appearance in great force on the trace [Santa Fe Trail]" (Wetmore 1832: 31).

Henry Dodge, explored along the foothills of the Rockies between the headwaters of the Platte and Arkansas Rivers, reported that the area was frequented by large parties of Blackfeet, Crows, Snakes, and sometimes Eutas [Utes], in addition to the Cheyennes and Arapahos who dominated the area (Dodge 1936: 22-23). When Dodge (1836: 25) got to Bent's Old Fort, on the Arkansas River, he "held a council with the Cheyennes, Arepahas, Gros-ventres, and a few Blackfeet." He commented that "The Gros-ventres of Fort du Prairie, now living with the Arepahas, are a band of the Blackfeet" and that they spoke the same language, had the same manners, and came from the same area, near the Forks of the Missouri River. Dodge reported that there were some 350 Blackfeet living among the Arapahos and that between 1824 and 1832 they had some 700 lodges. In 1842, Rufus Sage (1956: 68-69) encountered 15 lodges of Blackfeet with a much larger group of Arapahos near what is now Denver and, about 15 miles farther south, a group of Blackfeet camped under a large rock overhang. The territory, however, Sage ascribed to the Arapaho.

CHAPTER ELEVEN

THE CROWS

The Crow, a Siouan tribe that lived primarily on the Northern Plains, apparently moved there from the Middle Missouri River area early in historic times. Although the Crow were never a major tribe in the Central High Plains, some of them did get there from time to time. If, as D. Gunnerson (1983) has recently suggested, the Crows were called Aas by the New Mexicans, then they were known there, perhaps chiefly as captives, by the mid-1700s. This may have been one of the so-called "Nations of the North."

CHAPTER TWELVE
THE AAS

The identification of a tribe known to the New Mexicans as As, also rendered A, AA, Aa, aa, Aaa, and Haa (along with various diacritical marks) is uncertain. Bruge (1965) found reference to them in Church records going back to 1742 and continuing for a century. Simmons (1973) has suggested that the As were Skidi Pawnee, but his case is not sound. He considered his clinching evidence to be a parenthetical statement regarding a nation "the French call Ayoues and the Spaniards Aas" in a letter dated April 19, 1778, written by the Indian "Agent" [Athanase] De Mezieres (Pichardo 1931-1941 III: 243-244). However, the statement in question was merely an opinion inserted parenthetically by Pichardo and is not included in Bolton's translation of a letter written by De Mezieres to [the Marques de] Croix (Bolton 1914 II: 210) or in the original document (Archivo General, Provincias Internas, Vol. 182).

Recently D. Gunnerson (1983) has brought to bear various lines of evidence that lead to the conclusion that the As were Crows. Considering the range of spellings of the name, it could represent an attempt to render the cry of the crow bird. The Nahuatl (classical Aztec) name for the crow is "cacalotl." The initial "caca" is very close to "Aa" or "Haa." Many Nahuatl words came into common use in New Mexico during the 1600s. Furthermore, the Kiowa name for the Crow tribe is Gaa which shows up as a combining morpheme in several related words, and the Arikara name for their Crow clan includes the initial morpheme "kaka." Other lines of evidence cited by D. Gunnerson (1984) support the idea that Crows were indeed accustomed to travel from their northern plains homeland south to New Mexico.

In any case, the range of the Crows was primarily far to the north. In 1805 Francois Antoine Larocque, representing the owners of the Northwest Company of Canada, made a trip from the Assiniboine River to the Yellowstone River to visit the land of the "Rocky Mountain Savages," or Crow Indians, and to assess the possibility of trading for beaver pelts. Crow Indians were accustomed to come into the villages of the Mandan and Hidatsa, their linguistic relatives, who lived along the Missouri River in North Dakota. Apparently one of the Arikara chiefs was a Crow (Hazlitt 1934). In 1811 Henry Brackenridge (1814: 86) described the Crow Indians as being "divided into numerous tribes and scattered over the country on the heads of the Missouri and Yellowstone." He estimated their total population at 7,000. As an appendix, Brackenridge (1814: 297-302) included an account by Robert Steuart that had been

previously published in the *Missouri Gazette*, on June 28, 1812. Steuart and a small party were returning east from the Pacific via the Columbia River when they encountered a party of Crow Indians "within about 200 miles of the Rocky Mountains." In 1811, on their way west, they encountered "a band of the Absaroka or Crow nation" on the Powder River [Wyoming] at the foot of the Big Horn Mountain.

The Long party, in 1820, apparently did not meet any Crows but Bell, one of the leaders, learned that the Crow were made up of several wandering bands and that the Arapaho and Cheyennes traded with the Crow for items which that tribe, in turn, received from the Mandan, with whom European traders resided (Bell 1957: 202-204). While on the Arkansas River, near the mouth of the Purgatory, the party met a Badheart Indian (Kiowa Apache) and a woman who were on their way to join some Crows who were "residing somewhere in the region of the mountains" (Bell 1957: 180-186). Presumably neither the Indian nor the woman was Crow but they were taking refuge among them because the man had recently stolen the woman from her husband. In 1821 Jacob Fowler (Coues 1970: 59), while camped near the mouth of the Apishapa River within sight of the Rockies in southeastern Colorado, recorded in his journal that five days before there had been a battle near the mountains between the Crow and some other Indians, including at least one Arapaho. A few days later Fowler recorded that a party of Ietans (Comanches) returned with 28 horses taken from Crows "on the River Platt below the mountains" (Coues 1970: 63). Fowler, with the Hugh Glenn party, was camped at a rendezvous of some 700 tents of Kiowas, Kiowa Apaches, Cheyennes, Arapahos, and Shoshonis. A few weeks later, while the Glenn-Fowler party was still on the Arkansas River, but closer to the mountains, a party of 13 Crows with about 200 horses were met. The Crows had stolen the horses from some other tribe and were on their way to the Platte River where the rest of their nation resided. A party of Arapahos overtook the Crows and a battle ensued (Coues 1970: 70-71). The Crow were well aware that a major Indian trail followed the foot of the Rockies south to Spanish New Mexico and warned Fowler that he would be likely to be robbed if he continued to camp along it. The trail was called by the Blackfeet the "Old North Trail" (McClintock 1910).

Atkinson (1825: 11) noted that the Crows, who roamed from the Black Hills west to the Rocky Mountains, were at peace with the "Keawas and Arapahos, who reside on the headwaters of the Arkansas and Platte." This suggests at least contact by the Crows with tribes of the Central High Plains by that time.

In 1835 Henry Dodge (1836: 22-23) reported that large parties of Crows, Blackfeet, Snakes, and sometimes Utes, as well as Arapahos and Cheyennes, frequented the area east of the mountains between the Platte and Arkansas Rivers. Although various maps of the 1830s show the Crow on the north side of the Wind River, [Wyoming], on the 1836 map by Steen, who was with Dodge, one finds near the Rockies, just south of the South Platte River, the notation "Snake's and Crow's War Ground" (Wheat 1958 II: map 421). In 1845 Abert and Peck, while on the Canadian River, essentially straight north of Amarillo, met a party of Kiowas who were accompanied by a few Crows (Abert 1846: 42), thus recalling the strong Kiowa-Crow affinities reported by Mooney (1898). Hafen (1981: 296), citing a statement made by a reporter named Brown in 1851, characterized the Crows as: "tireless wanderers who ranged as far east as the Mandans, as far south as the Canadian River, through a great part of the West, and as far north as their implacable enemies, the Blackfeet, would let them!" They attended the Horse Creek Council on the North Platte River, near the Nebraska-Wyoming line, in 1851. "None of the tribe, he [Brown] wrote, 'had ever been so far east of their own grounds.'"

CHAPTER THIRTEEN

THE SIOUX

By the middle of the 1800s, the Sioux became a dominant power north of the Central High Plains, especially between the Black Hills and the Missouri River. The South Platte River was essentially the southern limit of Sioux territory, although Sioux were frequently found farther south, along with members of various other tribes.

In 1844 John C. Fremont (1845: 111) reported Sioux, along with Kiowas and Comanches, on the Arkansas River about 20 miles below Bent's Old Fort, near the present location of Las Animas, Colorado. In 1847, Thomas Fitzpatrick, Indian Agent for the Upper Platte Agency, reported that the Cheyennes, along with the Arapahos and Sioux: "occupy indiscriminately the whole country along the eastern base of the Rocky Mountains from the northern frontier of New Mexico up to the Missouri River" (Fitzpatrick 1848: 243). The next year, in 1848, Fitzpatrick learned of large encampments of Sioux on the South Platte. He contacted them in early summer (Hafen 1981: 261). In 1850 Fitzpatrick, at his own request, met with Sioux, Cheyennes, Arapahos, Kiowas, and Kiowa Apaches on the Arkansas River where the Santa Fe Trail crossed it in what is now southwest Kansas (Hafen 1981: 277). The next year, however, the Sioux were apparently not among a gathering of the other tribes (plus the Comanches) in the same general area (Hafen 1981: 277, 280).

In the summer of 1851, Fitzpatrick proceeded from the Arkansas to Fort Laramie, on the South Platte River in southwestern Wyoming, where many Sioux, along with Cheyennes, Arapahos, and Shoshonis assembled. The large gathering soon exhausted the pasture so the group moved down the South Platte to Horse Creek. There it was joined by a large party of Crows and a few representatives of several other tribes. Here the Fort Laramie or Horse Creek Treaty was drafted, defining hunting territories for the various tribes and providing for passage of Europeans through this territory along the Oregon Trail. There were perhaps 10,000 Indians present although estimates ran as high as 60,000 (Hafen 1981: 284-301). Unfortunately, the U.S. Senate substantially amended the treaty before it was ratified so that it was not as favorable to the natives as was the document agreed to by the participating chiefs and by Thomas Fitzpatrick who represented the United States (Berthrong 1963: 118-123; Hafen 1981; 284-301). The amended treaty did not provide the intended protection to the Indians. For example, a large Cheyenne camp east of Fort Larned in west-central Kansas was destroyed by General Hancock in 1867 even though the Cheyenne were clearly within the territory agreed upon in the Fort Laramie Treaty (Otto *et al* 1867: 84-112). A significant number of Sioux were among the Cheyenne in this village. A few days earlier one village was reported to have two hundred lodges of Cheyennes and ten lodges of Sioux with a much larger village of Sioux nearby (Berthrong 1963: 273-279).

From the middle of the 1800s on, groups of Sioux were repeatedly mentioned as allied with both the northern Cheyenne in the Black Hills area and the southern Cheyenne as far south as western Oklahoma, but mainly north of the Arkansas River (Berthrong 1963; Grinnell 1956). Apparently in 1865 Sioux were actively recruited by Cheyennes to move south with them to fight against European settlers (Berthrong 1963: 245). Since Sioux were with the Cheyenne at their main village on the South Canadian, near Antelope Hills, in October 1868 (Berthrong 1963: 321), some of these Sioux were presumably involved in the Battle of the Washita River which took place the next month.

In October 1868, General Carr was engaged by a group of Sioux and Cheyenne on Beaver [Sappa] Creek, a southern tributary of the Republican River, near what is now the Kansas-Colorado line. A large band of Sioux wintered that year on the Republican and were joined by a sizable number of Cheyennes. In May of 1869, Carr set to flight a group of Sioux and destroyed their camp just south of the Republican River near the southwestern corner of Nebraska. Carr followed the trail of the Sioux north and encountered them again on Spring Creek, a northern tributary of the Republican southwest of Fort Kearney [Nebraska] (King 1963: 82, 94-99).

The Sioux were traditional enemies of the Pawnee and frequently attacked them. For example, in 1843 a party of Sioux attacked a Pawnee village on the Loup River at Plum creek, near Genoa, Nebraska and burned over half of the lodges (Carlton 1943: 107). In 1873, a group of Dakota Sioux attacked a Pawnee hunting party on a tributary of the Republican River near Trenton, Nebraska and routed them completely. This disastrous defeat of the Pawnee probably had much to do with their giving up their reservation on the Loup River in eastern Nebraska and moving to a reservation in Oklahoma where they would not be threatened by Sioux attack (Wedel 1936: 23).

ESSAY ON SOURCES

The ethnohistory of the Central High Plains is based on a variety of documentary sources and, particularly for the earlier periods, requires careful interpretation of data that are usually minimal, sometimes faulty, and often ambiguous. Most groups or tribes were known by a variety of names, those known to any one explorer dependent upon his own language, previous contacts, and upon the date recorded. Usually the name applied to a particular group of people was not the name by which they called themselves. Until the 1700s most of the information on the Central High Plains came from Spanish sources. In the late 1600s and the 1700s, information from French sources increased as France explored Louisiana and made deliberate efforts to trade in New Mexico. Late in the 1700s and into early the 1800s, Spain made a belated attempt to explore the Upper Missouri, but after 1804 information is primarily from American sources. By the end of the 1800s all the tribes that had once lived in the Central High Plains were put on reservations, none of which, strangely enough, is located within that area.

Many of the most useful documents are accounts of expeditions that set out to deliberately explore or to collect information. Often these were official parties, frequently quasi-military, whose leaders had to file reports of their direct observations on the geography and people met, while collecting hearsay information obtained from Indians and trappers. Maps were sometimes compiled by such parties and many included and/or perpetuated erroneous information. Government and church records, including correspondence, diaries, logs of daily activities and transcripts of trials or testimonies are also a useful source of information. Fortunately, many such documents are preserved in archives, some of which have been indexed, and some of which are available on microfilm or photocopy. A limited number of important documents have been published, but often only in translation. In recent decades the testimonies presented in Indian Land Claims cases have brought together substantial amounts of ethnohistorical information on various tribes, but all too often only sources published in English have been utilized.

In considering the ethnohistory of the high plains, one must keep the time dimension clearly in mind. The earliest eye-witness accounts are about two hundred years earlier in the southern two-thirds of the area than in the northern third. Also, many tribes known in the mid-1800s, when the entire Central High Plains had emerged into history, had arrived there at different times, and some of the groups that were in the area in early historic times had already been forced out. It is something of a paradox that we have documentary information for groups in the area in the 1500s and early 1600s for whom we have been unable to identify archaeological sites. Furthermore, with the influx of trade goods, very few camp sites within this area dating from the last half of the 1700s and the 1800s have been identified as to tribe. It will probably never be possible to define archaeological assemblages with enough precision to identify as to tribe most sites occupied in the Central High Plains after A.D. 1750.

There are a number of excellent guides to the ethnohistorical documents bearing on the Central High Plains. Although Twitchell's brief description of each of the documents frequently does not do justice to the content, his monumental guide to the Spanish Archives of New Mexico is probably the most useful single research tool for the pre-1821 period (Twitchell 1914). Fortunately, these documents can now be purchased on microfilm from the New Mexico State Archives and Records Center in Santa Fe. They are in two "volumes," corresponding to the two volumes of Twitchell's guide, a total of 32 reels, and include over 3000 documents. Twitchell's guide, which was republished by Arno Press in New York in 1976, does not include mention of many of the tribes dealt with in the documents, and the index to the guide does not include many of the tribes mentioned in the descriptions. Unfortunately, there are gaps in the Spanish Archives of New Mexico where documents have been destroyed, lost, or stolen. A few of the missing documents are now in the Bancroft Library at the University of California, Berkeley. Microfilm of these documents can be borrowed on interlibrary loan, but with the stipulation that the microfilm not be copied. A guide to these documents, called "New Mexico Originals," was published by Angelico Chavez in 1950. Recently the Mexican Archives of New Mexico (1821-1846) have been microfilmed by the State of New Mexico Records Center. These 43 reels can also be purchased at a reasonable price. A calendar was published in 1970, but the descriptions are so brief that they are of little help in trying to find information on specific tribes or even on Indian affairs. Another important reference tool is Bolton's (1913) *Guide to Materials for the History of the United States in the Principal Archives of Mexico*. Here, too, the published descriptions of the documents do not do justice to the scope of the information included. The Archivo General y Publico de la Nacion in Mexico, D.F. is very accommodating in providing, at a reasonable price, microfilm of any of its documents. One can order copies using Bolton's designations. Unfortunately, a few of the documents have been lost since the guide was published.

There are photocopies and transcripts of various of these documents in several research libraries in the United States that have strong Latin American holdings.

The richest single source of ethnohistorical data for the Central High Plains in the 1800's is to be found in numerous letters, reports, etc. which were generated through the U.S. War Department and published as House or Senate Documents. Frequently the titles of the individual documents will provide clues as to which will be useful for a particular area or tribe. Many of these official government documents, along with other publications, have recently been made available on microfilm under the title of *Western Americana; Frontier History of the Trans-Mississippi West, 1550-1900*. This was produced by Research Publications, Inc., 12 Lunar Drive, P.O. Box 3903, New Haven, Conn. 06525. The originals of most of the items microfilmed are in either the Yale University Libraries or the Newberry Library, Chicago. A published guide contains copies of standard library catalog cards for each item and there is an index in a separate volume. The edition includes some 6300 items on 617 reels.

Some standard reference tools that should not be overlooked include *An Ethnographic Bibliography of North America*. The most recent multivolume edition includes the Plains and the Southwest in the same volume (Murdock and O'Leary 1975, Vol. 5). The published catalog of the Peabody Museum Library at Harvard University is also an excellent guide. The old *Handbook of American Indians*, Bureau of American Ethnology, Bulletin No. 30, should neither be over-looked nor blindly accepted, and once the plains volume of its successor appears, it too should be consulted.

An important cartographic reference is Wheat's (1958) *Mapping the Transmississippi West, 1540-1861*. Volumes I and II, which go up to 1845, are especially useful. Unfortunately, the reproductions of many of the maps are poor and some are illegible. Some of the maps in the two atlases that accompany *Indian Tribes of the Illinois Country* (Tucker 1942; Temple 1975), published by the Illinois State Museum, cover the Central High Plains and are, in general, of good quality. One of the best guides to maps of the area, although it does not include reproductions of maps, is the *Descriptive List of Maps of Spanish Possessions in the United States, 1502-1829* compiled by Lowery (1912). Most of the maps described are in the Library of Congress. Photostats of these are available and can be ordered by the Lowery number.

Accounts of exploration in the Central High Plains are also included in the multivolume set of *Early Western Travels*, edited by R.G. Thwaites. Another frequently cited source is the six volumes of documents and excerpts edited by Margry (1875-1886) entitled *Decouvertes et etablissements des Francais dans l'ouest et dans le sud de l'Amerique septentrionale (1614-1754) memoires et documents originaux*. Presumably there are many errors in this edition and most of the documents deal with areas to the east of that being discussed.

A very useful reference is a description of all of the Military posts, forts, etc. in the *Military Division of the Missouri* (Sheridan 1872). Although by 1872 many of the posts that once existed had been abandoned, this publication gives accurate locations and descriptions of installations then extant in the plains and surrounding areas. Military reports and correspondence often refer to particular posts without giving information as to their locations. In addition to Military Posts, the various Indian reservations are listed, along with the tribes involved, the names of the agents, the size and population of each reservation, and the dates of treaties or laws establishing them. The accompanying map shows the locations of the posts, reservations, and Military districts from just east of the Mississippi River to the Pacific Ocean.

Another useful source is a list of Military Engagements between 1868 and 1882 in the plains and surrounding areas (Sheridan 1882). These are listed chronologically and each is described in varying detail. Frequently however, the tribal identification of the Indians is not given and there is no index or guide.

BIBLIOGRAPHY

Abel, Annie H. Ed.
1915   *The Official Correspondence of James S. Calhoun.* Washington: U.S. Government Printing Office.

Abel, Annie H.
1939   *Tabeau's Narrative of Loisel''s Expedition to the Upper Missouri* . University of Oklahoma Press, Norman.

1941   "Indian Affairs in New Mexico Under the Administration of William Carr Lane, from the Journal of John Ward." *New Mexico Historical Review* , vol. 16, pp. 202-232.

Abert J.J.
1846   *Communicating a report of an expedition led by Lieutenant Abert, on the upper Arkansas and through the country of the Comanche Indians in the fall of the year 1845.* Senate Doc., 20th Congress, 1st Session; no. 438.

Adams, E.B.
1953   "Notes and Documents Concerning Bishop Crespo's Visitation, 1730." *New Mexico Historical Review,* vol. 28, pp. 222-233.

Allen, Paul (Ed.)
1814   *History of the Expedition Under the Command of Lewis and Clark* .... 2 vols. Philadelphia.

Atkinson, Henry
1826   *....Expedition up the Missouri: Letter from the Secretary of War, transmitting information....regarding the movements of the expedition which lately ascended the Missouri River....*House Doc. U.S. 19th Congress, 1st Session, no. 117 Washington.

Ayer, Mrs. Edward, Tr.
1916   *The Memorial of Fray de Benevides, 1630.* Privately Printed. Chicago.

Bandelier, Adolph F.
1890   "Investigations Among the Indians of the Southwestern United States, Carried On Mainly In the Years From 1880-1885." *Papers of the Archaeological Institute of America.* American Series III, part 1. Peabody Museum of American Archaeology and Ethnology, Harvard University, Cambridge.

1892   "Final Report of Investigations Among the Indians of the Southwestern United States, Carried on Mainly In the Years From 1880-1885." *Papers of the Archaeological Institute of America,* series IV, part II. Peabody Museum of American Archaeology and Ethnology Harvard University, Cambridge.

Bannon, John F. (Ed.)
1964   *Bolton and the Spanish Borderlands.* University of Oklahoma Press, Norman.

Barry, Louise
1972   *The Beginning of the West, Annals of the Kansas Gateway to the American West, 1540-1854.* Kansas State Historical Society, Topeka.

Baugh, Timothy G.
1982   "Edwards I (34 BK 2): Southern Plains Adaptation In the Proto-Historic Period." Oklahoma Archaeological Survey. *Studies in Oklahoma's Past.* no. 8, Norman.

Beckwith, E.G.
1855   *Report of exploration of a route for the Pacific railroad, near the 38th and 39th parallels of latitude, from the mouth of the Kansas to Sevier River in the Great Basin.* U.S. War Department Report, 33rd Congress, 1st Session, House Ex. Doc 129, Washington.

Beidleman, Richard G.
1958   "A Partial, Annotated Bibliography of Colorado Ethnology." *The Colorado College Studies,* Fall, no. 2.

Bell, John R.
1957   *The journal of Captain John R. Bell, official journalist for the Stephen H. Long expedition to the Rocky Mountains, 1820.* H.M. Fuller and L.R. Hafen, Eds., Far West and Rockies Series, vol. VI. Glendale, CA.

Bell, Robert E., Edward B. Jelks, and W.W. Newcomb
1967   "A Pilot Study of Wichita Indian Archaeology and Ethnohistory." National Science Foundation, final report.

1974   *Wichita Indians: Wichita Indian Archaeology and Ethnology, A Pilot Study.* Garland Publishing Inc., New York & London.

Berthrong, Donald J.
1963   *The Southern Cheyennes.* University of Oklahoma Press, Norman.

Bolton, Herbert E.
1913a   "New Light on Manuel Lisa and the Spanish Fur Trade."*Southwestern Historical Quarterly,* Texas State Historical Association, vol. XVII, no. 1, pp. 61-66.

Bolton, Herbert E.

    1913b   *Guide to the Material for the History of the United States in the Principal Archives of Mexico* Carnegie Institution of Washington, Publication 163.

    1914   *Athanase de Mezieres and the Louisiana-Texas Fronties, 1768-1780.* 2 volumes. The Arthur H. Clark Company, Cleveland.

    1915   "Texas in the Middle Eighteenth Century." In: *University of California Publications in History*, vol III, H.M. Stephens and H.E. Bolton, Eds., Berkeley.

    1917   "French Instrusions into New Mexico, 1749-1752." In: *The Pacific Ocean in History*. Panama-Pacific Historical Congress, 1915, pp. 389-407. H.M. Stephens and H.E. Bolton Eds. The Macmillan Co., New York.

Brackenridge, Henry M.

    1814   *Views of Louisiana, Together with a Journal of a Voyage Up the Missouri River in 1811.* Pittsburgh.

Bradbury, John

    1817   *Travels in the Interior of American in the Years 1809,1810, and 1811.* Liverpool and London.

Brown, Kenneth

    1976   "Prehistoric cultural resources of the Cimarron National Grassland, Morton and Stevens counties, Kansas." Report submitted to USDA, Forest Service, Cimarron National Grassland District, Elkhart, Kansas.

Brugge, David M.

    1965   "Some Plains Indians in the Church Records of New Mexico." *Plains Anthropolgist*, vol. 10, no. 29, pp. 181-189.

    1968   "Navajos in the Catholic Church Records of New Mexico, 1694-1875." The Navajo Tribe, Parks and Recreation Department, *Research Report* no. 1. Window Rock, Arizona.

    1979   "Navajo Prehistory and History to 1850." Volume 10, *Handbook of North American Indians.* (William C. Sturtevant, General Ed.).

Bryan, Francis T.

    1857   *Exploration From Fort Riley to Bridger's Pass.* In: House Ex. Doc. 35th Congress, lst Session, no. 2, pp. 455-520, Washington.

Butler, William B.

    1980   "Comments on a research design for the state historic preservation plan; eastern Colorado." Paper presented at the March, 1980 meeting of the Colorado Council of Professional Archaeologists, in a symposium on Research Design and State Historic Preservation Plan.

Butler, P.M. and G.G. Lewis

    1846   *Report of Messrs. Butler & Lewis, Commissioners to Treat With the Comanchers and Other Praire Indians, Under Instructions from the War Department.* Washington.

Campbell, T.N.

    1960   "Texas Archaeology: A Guide to the Literature." *Bulletin of the Texas Archaeological Society*, vol. 29, pp. 177-254.

Carleton, J. Henry

    1943   *The Praire Logbooks, Dragoon Campaigns to the Pawnee Villages in 1844, and to the Rocky Mountains in 1845.* (Originally published in *Spirit of the Times*, New York, 1844-46). The Claxton Club, Chicago.

Carlson, Roy L.

    1965   *Eighteenth Century Navajo Fortresses of the Gobernador District.* University of Colorado Studies, Series in Anthropology 10. Boulder.

Carroll, H.B. and J.V. Haggard

    1942   *Three New Mexico Chronicles.* Quivira Society Publication no. 11.

Carroll, John M.

    1973   *The Sand Creek Massacre: A Documentary History.* New York.

Chavez, Fray Angelico

    1950   "Some Original New Mexico Documents in California Libraries." *New Mexico Historical Review*, vol 25, pp. 244-253.

Chronic, John and Halka

    1972   *Prairie, Peak and Plateau: A Guide to the Geology of Colorado.* Colorado Geological Survey Bulleting 32.

Clark, Tim W.

    1969   *Some Petroglyphs From the Black Mesa Area of Cimnaron County, Oklahoma.* Proceedings of the Oklahoma Academy of Science, 138-141.

Clements, F.E. and R.W. Chaney

    1937   *Environment and Life in the Great Plains.* Carnegie Institution of Washington, Supplementary Publications, no. 24 (rev. ed.).

Clements, Frederick E.
1938   "Climatic Cycles and Human Populations in the Great Plains." *Scientific Monthly*, vol. XLVII, no. 3, pp. 193-210.

Collins, Michael B.
1968   "A note on broad corner-notched projectile points used in bison hunting in western Texas." *The Bull Roarer, Newsletter of the University of Texas Anthropological Society*, vol. 3, no 2, pp. 13-14, Austin.

1971   "A Review of Llano Estacaso Archaeology and Ethnohistory." *Plains Anthropologist*, vol. 16, no. 52, pp. 85-104.

Cook, H.J.
1927   "New Geological and Paleontological Evidence Bearing on the Antiquity of Mankind in America." *Natural History*, vol. 7, no. 3, pp. 240-247

Cordell, Linda S.
1978   "A cultural resources overview of the middle Rio Grande Valley, New Mexico." For: Albuquerque District, Bureau of Land Management, and Carson National Forest, Cibola National Forest, Santa Fe National Forest, USDA Forest Service.

Coues, Elliott, Ed.
1895   *The Expedition of Zebulon Montgomery Pike to Headwaters of the Mississippi river, Through Louisiana Territory and New Spain, During the Years 1806-7.* New York.

1965   *History of the Expedition Under the Command of Lewis and Clark in Three Volumes.* (Republication of Harper 1893 edition). Dover Publications, New York.

1970   *The Journal of Jacob Fowler.* University of Nebraska Press, Lincoln.

Cutler, Hugh C. and Leonard W. Blake
1969   'Corn.' In: "Two House Sites In the Central Plains: An Experiment In Archaeology," Ed. by W. Raymond Wood. *Plains Anthropologist*, vol 14, no. 44, pt. 2, pp. 61-62.

Dodge, Henry
1834   *[Journal of Colonel Dodge's expedition from Fort Gibson to the Pawnee Pict Village.]* Senate Doc., 23rd Congress, 2nd Session, no. 1. Washington.

1836   .... *Colonel Dodge's Journal* .... *Report to the Secretary of War....Transmitting a Report of the Expedition of the Dragoons, Under the Command of Colonel Henry Dodge, to the Rocky Mountains During the Summer of 1835.* House Doc. [U.S.] 24th Congress, 1st Session, no. 181, Washington.

Douglas, F.H.
1932   *The Grass House of the Wichita and Caddo.* Denver Art Museum, Indian Leaflet Series, no. 42, pp. 1-4.

Duffield, Lathel F.
1965   "The Taovayas Village of 1759: In Texas or Oklahoma?" *Great Plains Journal*, vol. 4, no. 2, pp. 39-48.

Du Lac, Perrin
1807   *Travels Through the Two Louisianas, 1801, 1802, 1803.* London.

Dunbar, John B.
1835   "Extracts From the Journal of Mr. Dunbar." *The Missionary Herald For 1835*, vol. 31, pp. 343-349, 376-381, 417-421.

1880   "The Pawnee Indians: Their History and Ethnology." *Magazine of American History*, vol. 4, no. 4, pp. 241-281.

1911   "Missionary Life Among the Pawnee." *Collections of the Nebraska State Historical Society*, vol. XVI, pp. 268-287. Albert Watkins, Ed.

Ekirch, Arthur A., Jr.
1974   "Cheyenne and Arapaho Indians." *American Indian Ethnohistory, Plains Indians, Arapaho-Cheyenne Indians.* Garland Publishing Co. New York and London.

Emory, W.H.
1848   *Notes of a Military Reconnaissance from Fort Levenworth, in Missouri to San Diego, in California, Including Part of the Arkansas, Del Norte, and Gila Rivers.* Senate Ex. Doc. 30th Congress, 1st Session, no. 7, Washington.

Espinosa, J. Manuel
1942   *Crusaders of the Rio Grande.* Institute of Jesuit History Publications. Chicago.

Ewers, John C., and Stuart Cuthbertson
1939   "A preliminary bibliography on the American fur trade." Report on file, National Park Service, Midwest Archaeological Center, Lincoln, Nebraska.

Ewers, John C.
1958   *The Blackfeet: Raiders of the Northwestern Plains.* University of Oklahoma Press, Norman.

Field, Mathew C.
    1957   *Prairie and Mountain Sketches.* K. Gregg and J. Mc Dermott. Eds. University of Oklahoma Press, Norman.

Fisher, William (Comp.)
    1812   *New Travels Among the Indians of North America: Being A Compliation, Taken Partly from the Communications Already Published, of Captains Lewis and Clark to the President of the United States, and Partly From Other Authors who Travelled Among Various Tribes of Indians ....* Philadelphia.

Fitzgerald, James E.
    1849   *An Examination of the Character and Proceedings of the Hudson's Bay Company, With Reference to the Grant of Vancouver's Island.* London

Fitzpatrick, Thomas
    1848   [Report, as Indian Agent to the Superintendent of Indian Affairs.] In: U.S. President 1845-1849 (Polk). Message December 7, 1847, Appendix, pp. 237-249. Washington. Also: Senate Ex. Doc. U.S. 30th Congress, 1st Session, no 1, Serial 503, pp. 237-249.

Fletcher, Alice C.
    1907   "Grass houses." In: *Handbook of American Indians.* Bulleting 30 Bureau of American Ethnology, Pt. 1, Washington.

Folmer, Henri
    1939   "The Mallet Expedition of 1739 Through Nebraska, Kansas and Colorado to Santa Fe." *Colorado Magazine,* vol. XVI, (September) pp. 1-13.

    1939   "French Expansion Towards New Mexico in the Eighteenth Century." Unpublished M.A. Thesis, University of Denver.

    1953   "Franco-Spanish Rivalry in North America." *Spain in the West,* vol. VII, A.H. Clark Co., Glendale, Ca.

Forbes, Jack D.
    1960   *Apache, Navajo and Spaniard.* University of Oklahoma Press, Norman.

Foreman, Grant
    1926   *Pioneer Days in the Early Southwest.* A.H. Clark Co., Cleveland.

    1933   *Advancing the Frontier. 1830-1860.* University of Oklahoma Press, Norman.

Forman, Grant (Ed.)
    1937   *Adventure on Red River. Report of the Exploration of the Headwaters of the Red River by Captain Randolph B. Marcy and Captain G.B. Mc Clellan.* University of Olkahoma Press Norman.

Fremont, John C.
    1843   *A Report of an Exploration of the Country Lying Between the Missouri River and the Rocky Mountains on the Line of the Kansas and Great Platte Rivers....* U.S. 27th Congress 3rd Session, Sen. Doc. 243. Washington

    1845   *Report of the Exploring Expedition to the Rocky Mountains in the Year 1842 and to Oregon and North California in the Years 1843-1844.* U.S. 28tb Congress, 2nd Session, Senate Ex. Doc. 174. Washington.

    1887   *Memoirs of My Life, Including the Narrative Five Journeys of Western Exploration, During the Years 1842, 1843-44, 1845-46-47, 1848-49, 1853-54.* Chicago and New York.

Frost, Lawrence
    1960   "Battle of the Washita." In: *Great Western Indian Fights.* By Members of the Potomac Corral of the Westerners. Pp. 175-181. Garden City, NY.

Fuller, H.M. and L.R. Hafen Eds.
    1957   *The Journal of Captain John R. Bell...1820.* Far West and Rockies Series, vol. VI, Glendale, CA.

Gardner, Hamilton
    1963   "Philip St. George Cooke and the Apache, 1854." *New Mexico Historical Review,* vol 28. pp. 115-132.

Ghent, W.J.
    1936   *The Early Far West.* Tudor Publishing Co., New York.

Goddard, Pliny E.
    1911   "Jicarilla Apache Texts." American Museum of Natural History Papers, 8.

Grange, Roger T. Jr.
    1968   "Pawnee and Lower Loup Pottery." Nebraska State Historical Society, *Publications in Anthropology,* no. 3, Lincoln

    1976   "An Archaeological View of Pawnee Origins." *Nebraska History,* vol. 60, no. 2, pp. 134-160.

Grant, Blanche C.
    1934   *When Old Trails Were New, The Story of Taos.* Press of the Pioneers, New York.

Grinnell, G.B.
    1915   *The Fighting Cheyennes.* New York.

1956   *The Fighting Cheyennes.* (Published in 1915 by Charles Scribner's Sons) University of Oklahoma Press, Norman.

Gunnerson, Dolores A.

1956   "The Southern Athabascans: Their Arrival in the Southwest." *El Palacio,* vol. 63, nos. 11-12, pp. 346-365.

1972   "Man and Bison on the Plains in the Protohistoric Period." *Plains Anthropologist,* vol. 17, no. 55, pp. 1-1.

1974   *The Jicarilla Apaches: A Study in Survival.* Northern Illinois University Press, DeKalb, Illinois.

1984a   "Indian 'Nations of the North' on the New Mexico Spanish Frontier." Paper presented at the 1984 Nebraska Academy of Sciences. Lincoln.

1984b   "Padoucas: Apaches of the Paddocks." Paper presented at the annual meeting of the New Mexico Archaeological Council, Cimarron, New Mexico.

Gunnerson, James H.

1959   "Archaeological Survey in Northeastern New Mexico." *El Palacio* vol. 66, no. 5, pp. 145-155. Santa Fe.

1960   "An Introduction to Plains Apache Archaeology—The Dismal River Aspect." Anthropological Paper No. 58, Smithsonian Institution, Bureau of American Ethnology, *Bulletin* 173, pp. 129-260. Washington.

1968   "Plains Apache Archaeology: A Review." *Plains Anthropologist,* vol. 13, no. 41, pp. 167-189.

1969a   "A Human Skeleton from an Apache Baking Pit." *Plains Anthropologist,* vol. 14, no. 43, pp. 46-56.

1969b   "Apache Archaeology in Northeastern New Mexico." *American Antiquity,* vol. 34, no. 1, pp. 23-39.

1973   Field Notes.

1979   "Southern Athapaskan Archaeology." In: *Handbook of North American Indians.* vol. 9, pp. 162-169. Smithsonian Institution, Washington.

1984   "Documentary Clues and Northeastern New Mexico Archaeology." Paper presented at the 1984 annual meeting of the New Mexico Archaeological Conference (in press).

1987   *Archaeology of the High Plains.* Bureau of Land Management, Denver, Colorado.

Gunnerson, James H. and Dolores A. Gunnerson

1970   "Evidence of Apaches at Pecos." *El Palacio,* vol, 76. pp. 1-6. "Apachean Culture: A Study in Unity and Diversity." In: *Apachean Culture History and Ethnology.* Keith H. Basso and Morris E. Opler, Eds. pp. 7-27. Tucson: Anthropological Papers of the University of Arizona, 21.

Gussow, Zachary

1974   "Cheyenne and Arapaho Aboriginial Occupation." In: *American Indian Ethnohistory, Plains Indians, Arapaho-Cheyenne Indians.* New York and London.

Hackett, Charles W., Trans. and Ed.

1923-1937   *Historical Documents Relating to New Mexico, Nueva Vizcaya and Approaches Thereto, to 1773.* 3 vols. Carnegie Institution of Washington, Publication 330. Washington.

1934-1946   *Pichardo's Treatise on the Limits of Louisana and Texas.* 4 vols. University of Texas Press.

Hafen, LeRoy R. and Ann W. Hafen (Eds.)

1955-1961   *Relations with the Indians of the Plains, 1857-1861.* The Far West and Rockies Historical Series, vol. IX, A.H. Clark, Glendale, CA.

Hafen, LeRoy (Ed.)

1966   *The Mountain Men and the Fur Trade of the Far West.* 8 vols. Glendale, CA.

Hafen, LeRoy R.

1974   "Historical Development of the Arapaho-Cheyenne Land Area." In: *American Indian Ethnohistory. Plains Indians, Arapaho-Cheyenne Indians.* New York and London.

1981   *Broken Hand: The Life of Thomas Fitzpatrick, Mountain Man, Guide and Indian Agent.* (Reprint of 1931 edition). University of Nebraska Press, Lincoln.

Hammond, George P. and Agapito Rey

1928   *Obregon's History of the 16th century Explorations in Western America.* Wetzel Publishing Co. Inc., Los Angeles.

1940   *Narratives of the Coronado Expedition, 1540-1542.* Coronado Historical Series, vol 2. University of New Mexico.

1953   *Don Juan de Onate, Colonizer of New Mexico, 1595-1628.* 2 vols. Albuquerque: University of New Mexico Press.

1966   *The Rediscovery of New Mexico, 1580-1594.* University of New Mexico Press, Albuquerque.

Harlow, Francis H.

1970   *Historic Pueblo Indian Pottery: Painted Jars and Bowls of the Period 1600-1900.* Santa Fe: Museum of New Mexico Press.

Hazlitt, Ruth, Ed.
    1934   *The Journal of Francois Antoine Larocque From the Assiniboine River to the Yellowstone-1805.* Historical Reprints, Sources of Northwest History, No. 20, State University of Montana, Missoula.

Hodge, F.W., Ed.
    1907-1910   Handbook of American Indians North of Mexico. Bureau of American Ethnology, Bulletin 30, 2 pts. Washington.

Hodge, F.W., G.P. Hammond and A. Rey.
    1945   *Fray Alonso de Benevides' Revised Memorial of 1634.* University of New Mexico Press, Albuquerque.

Hoijer, Harry
    1938   "The Southern Athapascan Languages." *American Anthropologist,* vol. 40, p. 74.

    1956   "The Chronology of the Athapaskan Languages." *International Journal of American Linguistics,* vol. 22, no. 4, pp. 219-232.

    1971   "The Position of the Apachean Languages in the Athapaskan Stock." In: *Apachean Culture History and Ethnology,* pp. 3-6. Keith Basso and Morris E. Opler, Eds. Anthropological Papers of the University of Arizona, 21, Tucson.

Huscher, Betty and Harold Huscher
    1943   "The Hogan Builders of Colorado." *Southwestern Lore,* vol. 9, no. 2.

Hyde, George E.
    1934a   *The Pawnee Indians, Part One,* 1500-1680. The Old West Series, no. 4. Denver.

    1934b   *The Pawnee Indians, Part Two,* 1680-1770. The Old West Series, no. 5. Denver.

    1951   *Pawnee Indians.* University of Denver Press, Denver.

Indian Claims Commission
    1957   "Findings, Cheyenne-Arapahoe Tribes of Indians, etc. *et al* vs. the United States of America." (1955-1961). In: *American Indian Ethnohistory, Plains Indians, Arapoho-Cheyenne Indians,* pp. 229-342. New York and London.

Irving, J.T.
    1835   *Indian Sketches.* 2 vols. Philadelphia.

    1955   *Indian Sketches Taken During and Expedition to the Pawnee Tribes.* University of Oklahoma Press, Norman.

Jablow, Joseph
    1950   *The Cheyenne in Plains Indian Trade Relations, 1795-1840.* Monographs of the American Ethnological Society, no. XIX, New York.

Jackson, A.T.
    1938   *Picture-Writing of Texas Indians.* University of Texas Publication no. 3809, Austin.

Jackson, Donald, Ed.
    1966   *The Journals of Zebulon Montgomery Pike.* 2 vols. University of Oklahoma Press, Norman.

James, Edwin, Comp.
    1822-1823   *Account of an Expedition from Pittburgh to the Rocky Mountains, Performed in the Year 1819 and 1820, by Order of the Hon. J.C. Calhoun, Sec'y. of War; Under the Command of Major Stephen H. Long....* 2 vol. and atlas. Philadelphia.

James, Thomas
    1916   *Three Years Among the Indians and Mexicans.* Ed. by Walter B. Douglas. Missouri Historical Society, St. Louis.

Jefferson, Thomas
    1806   *Message from the president of the United States communicating discoveries made in exploring the Missouri, Red River and Washita, by Captains Lewis and Clark, Doctor Sibley, and Mr. Dunbar; with a statistical account of the countries adjacent.* Washington, D.C.

Jett, Stephen C.
    1964   "Pueblo Indian Migrations: An Evaluation of the Physical and Cultural Determinants." *American Antiquity,,* vol. 29, no. 3, pp. 281-300.

John, Elizabeth A.H.
    1975   *Storms Brewed In Other Men's Worlds; The Confrontation of Indians, Spanish and French in the Southwest, 1540-1795.* Texas A&M University Press, College Station.

Keleher, William A.
    1964   *Maxwell Land Grant.* New York: Argosy-Antiquarian Ltd.

Kenner, Charles L.
    1969   *A History of New Mexican-Plains Indian Relations.* University of Oklahoma Press, Norman.

King, James T.
    1963   *War Eagle, A Life of General Eugene A. Carr.* University of Nebraska Press, Lincoln.

Kirkland, Forrest
    1942   "Indian Pictographs and Petroglyphs in the Panhandle Region of Texas." *Bulletin of the Texas Archaeological and Paleontological Society*, vol. 14, pp. 9-26.

Kirkland, Forrest, and W.W. Newcomb, Jr.
    1967   *The Rock Art of the Texas Indians*. The University of Texas Press, Austin.

Krause, Richard A.
    1969   'Correlation of Phases in Central Plains Prehistory' In: "Two Hourse Sites in the Central Plains: An Experiment in Archaeology," W.R. Wook Ed., *Plains Anthropologist*, Memoir 6, pp. 82-96.

    1970   "Aspects of Adaptation Among Upper Republican Subsistence Cultivators." In: *Pleistocene and Recent Environments of the Central Great Plains*, Wakefield Dort, Jr. and J. Knox Jones, Jr., Eds. Department of Geology, University of Kansas, Special Publication, 3, pp. 103-116.

Lang, Richard W.
    1977   "The Prehistoric Pueblo Cultural Sequence in the Northern Rio Grande." School of American Research. Paper Presented at the 1977 Pecos Conference. Santa Fe.

    1982   'Transformation in White Ware Pottery of the Northern Rio Grande,' In: "Southwestern Ceramics: A Comparative View," *The Arizona Archaeologist*, no. 15, pp. 153-200.

Lavender, David
    1954   *Bent's Fort*. University of Nebraska Press, Lincoln.

Lewis, [Meriwether]
    1814   *History of the Expedition Under the Command of Captains Lewis and Clark, to the Sources of the Missouri, Thence Across the Rocky Mountains, and Down the River Columbia to the Pacific Ocean. Performed During the Years 1804-1805-1806*. Prepared for the press by Paul Allen, Esq. 2 vols. Philadelphia and New York.

Lewis, M. and Wm. Clark
    1904   *Original Journals of the Lewis and Clark Expedition, 1804-1806*. R.G. Thwaits, Ed. New York.

Lewis, Sol
    1973   The Sand Creek Massacre, A Documentary History. New York.

Loomis, Noel M. and Abraham P. Nasatir
    1967   *Pedro Vial and the Roads to Santa Fe*. University of Oklahoma Press, Norman.

Lowery, Woodbury
    1912   *The Lowery Collection, A Descriptive List of Maps of the Spanish Possessions Within the Present Limits of the United States, 1502-1820*. Washington.

Ludwickson, John
    1975   "The Loup River Phase and the Origins of Pawnee Culture." M.A. Thesis, University of Nebraska, Lincoln.

    1978   "Central Plains Tradition Settlements in the Loup River Basin: The Loup River Phase." pp. 94-105. In: *The Central Plains Tradition: Internal Development and External Relationships*, Donald J. Blakeslee, Ed., Report no. 11, Office of the State Archaeologist, Iowa City.

Luttig, John C.
    1964   *Journal of a Fur-Trading Expedition on the Upper Missouri, 1812-1813*. Stella A. Drumm, Ed. Argosy-Antiquarian Ltd., New York.

McCall, George A.
    1851   *Report of the Secretary of War, Communicating, in Compliance With A Resolution of the Senate, Colonel McCall's Reports in Relation to New Mexico, February 10, 1851*. Senate Ex. Doc. 31st Congress, 2nd Session, no. 26. Washington.

McClintock, Walter
    1968   *The Old North Trail, or Life, Legends, and Religion of the Blackfeet Indians*. University of Nebraska Press, Lincoln. (Originally published in 1910).

McDermott, John F.
    1965   *The French in the Mississippi Valley*. University of Illinois Press, Urbana.

    1974   *The Spanish in the Mississippi Valley, 1762-1804*. University of Illinois Press, Urbana.

Marcy, Randolph B.
    1853   *Exploration of the Red River of Louisiana in the Year 1853*. Senate Ex. Doc., 32nd Congress, 2nd Sess., no 54, Washington.

    1856   *...The Report and Maps of Captain Marcy of His Explorations of the Big Wichita and Headwaters of the Brazos Rivers*. Sen. Ex. Doc., 34th Congress, 1st Session, no. 60.

Margry, Pierre
　　1875-1886　　　*Decouveretes et Establissements de Francais dan l' Quest de dans le Sud de l' Amerique Septentrionale (1614-1754).*
　　　　　　　　　　　Memoires et Doucements Originaux. 6 vols. Paris.

Martin, H.T.
　　1909　　　"Further Notes on the Pueblo Ruins of Scott County." *Kansas University Science Bulletin*, vol. 5, no. 2, pp. 11-
　　　　　　　12.

Millbrook, Minnie Dubbs
　　1973　　　"Custer's First Scout in the West." *Kansas Historical Quarterly*, vol. 39, pp. 75-95.

Miller, Nyle H.
　　1977　　　"The Annual Meeting, Report of the Executive Director, Year Ending October 19, 1976," *Kansas Historical Quarterly*,
　　　　　　　vol. 43, no. 1, pp. 78-98.

Minge, Ward Alan
　　1979　　　"Efectos del Pais: A History of Weaving Along the Rio Grande." In: *Spanish Textile Tradition of New Mexico and
　　　　　　　Colorado*, pp. 8-28, Museum of International Folk Art, Santa Fe.

Mooney, James
　　1896　　　"The Ghost-Dance Religion and the Sioux Outbreak of 1890." Bureau of American Ethnology. *Annual Report*, no.
　　　　　　　14, pt. 2. Washington.

　　1898　　　"Calendar History of the Kiowa Indians." Bureau of American Ethnology. *Annual Report*, no. 17, pt. 1, pp. 129-
　　　　　　　445.

Morse, Jedidiah
　　1822　　　*A Report to the Secretary of War of the United States, on Indian Affairs, Comprising a Narrative of a Tour Performed
　　　　　　　in the Summer of 1820.* New Haven.

Moulton, Gary E.
　　1983　　　*Atlas of the Lewis and Clark Expedition. The Journal of the Lewis and Clark Expedition.* vol. 1, University of Nebraska
　　　　　　　Press, Lincoln.

Mulloy, William T.
　　1958　　　*A Preliminary Historical Outline for the Northwestern Plains.* University of Wyoming Publications, vol. 22, pp. 1-
　　　　　　　235.

Murdock, George P. and Timothy J. O'Leary
　　1975　　　*Ethnographic Bibliography of North America*, vol. 5, *Plains and Southwest.* (4th Ed.) HRAF Press, New Haven.

Murray, Charles A.
　　1839　　　*Travels in North American During the Years 1834, 1835, and 1836: Including a Summers Residence with the Pawnee
　　　　　　　Tribe of Indians....* 2 vols., London.

Nasatir, A.P.
　　1952　　　*Before Lewis and Clark, Documents Illustrating the History of the Missouri, 1785-1804.* 2 vols. St. Louis Historical
　　　　　　　Documents Foundation.

　　1974　　　"More on Pedro Vial in Upper Louisiana." In: *The Spanish in the Mississippi Valley, 1762-1804.* F.J. McDermott,
　　　　　　　Ed., pp. 100-119. University of Illinois Press, Urbana.

Newcomb, W.W.
　　1961　　　*The Indians of Texas From Prehistoric to Modern Times.* University of Texas Press, Austin.

Oehler, Gottlieb and David Smith
　　1851　　　"Description of a Journey and Visit to the Pawnee Indians, April 22 - May 18, 1851." *Moravian Church Miscellany*,
　　　　　　　1851-52.

　　1914　　　*Description of a Journey and Visit to the Pawnee Indians.* New York.

Opler, Morris E.
　　1938　　　*Myths and Tales of the Jicarilla Apache Indians.* American Folklore Society, Memoir 31.

Otto, W.T., *et al*
　　1867　　　*Letter of the Secretary of the Interior Communicating... Information Touching the Origin and Progress of Indian
　　　　　　　Hostilities on the Frontier.* Senate Ex. Doc., no. 13, 40th Congress, 1st Session.

Parks, Douglas R.
　　1979　　　"The Northern Caddoan Languages: Their Subgrouping and Time Depth." *Nebraska History*, vol. 60, no. 2, pp.
　　　　　　　197-213.

Peabody Museum
　　1963　　　*Catalog of the Library of the Peabody Museum of Archaeology and Ethnology, Harvard University.* 53 vols. plus
　　　　　　　1970-71 supplements. 17 vols., G.K. Hall and Co., Boston.

Perrin du Lac, Francois Marie
 1805 *Voyage dans le Deux Louisianes, et Chez les Nations Sauvages du Missouri...en 1801, 1802 et 1803...a Lyon.*

 1807 *Travels Through the Two Louisianas, and Among the Savage Nations of the Missouri...in 1801, 1802, and 1803....* Tr. from the French. London.

Pope, John
 1855 *Report of Exploration of a Route for the Pacific Railroad, Near the Thirty-Second Parallel of Latitude, From the Red River to the Rio Grande.* House Ex. Doc. 129, 33rd Congress, 1st Session.

Raczka, Paul M.
 1972 "Traditions of Northern Plains Raiders in New Mexico." El Corral de Santa Fe Westerners, *Brandbook, 1973.* pp. 49-53, Santa Fe.

Rathjen, Frederick W.
 1973 *The Texas Panhandle Frontier.* University of Texas Press, Austin .

Reid, Russell
 1965 "Verendrye's Journey to North Dakota in 1738." *North Dakota History,* vol. 32, no. 2, State Historical Society, Bismarck.

Renaud, E.B.
 1930 "Prehistoric Cultures of the Cimarron Valley, Northeastern New Mexico and Western Oklahoma." Colorado Scientific Society *Proceedings,* vol. 12, no. 5, pp. 113-150. Denver.

 1942 "Reconnaissance Work in the Upper Rio Grande Valley, Colorado and New Mexico." University of Denver, Department of Anthropology, *Archaeological Series,* 3rd Paper, Denver.

 1947 "Archaeology of the High Western Plains, 17 Years of Archaeological Research." Denver.

Russell, Frank
 1898 "Myths of the Jicarilla Apaches." *Journal of American Folklore,* vol. 11, pp. 253-271.

Sage, Rufus B.
 1965 *Scenes in the Rocky Mountains and in Oregon, California, New Mexico, Texas, and the Grand Priairies.* Reprinted in Far West and Rockies Series, vols. 4 and 5. Glendale, CA.

Schofield, J.M. et al
 1869 *Letter of the Secretary of War, Communicating... Information in Relation to the Late Indian Battle on the Washita River.* Senate E. Doc., 40th Congress, 3rd Session, no. 18.

Schroeder, Albert H.
 1959 "A Study of the Apache Indians." Part II, The Jicarilla Apaches. Mimeographed. Santa Fe, New Mexico.

Sheridan, P.H.
 1869 [Report to General W.T. Sherman of Action of the Military.] Division of Missouri, Chicago, Illinois, November 1, 1869.

 1872 U.S. Army. Military Division of the Missouri. *Outline Description of the Post in the Military Division of the Missouri...Accompanied by Tabular Lists of Indian Superintendencies, Agencies, and Reservations....* Chicago.

 1882 *Record of Engagements With Hostile Indians Within the Military Division of the Missouri, From 1868 to 1882.* Chicago, Ill.

Sibley, John et al
 1803[?] *An Account of Louisiana: Being an Abstract of Documents In the Offices of the Departments of State and of the Treasury.* Washington.

Simmons, Marc
 1973 "The Mysterious A Tribe of the Southern Plains." Corral de Santa Fe Westerners, *Brandbook, 1972.* pp. 73-89. Santa Fe.

Steen, C.R.
 1955 *A Survey of Archaeology and History in the Arkansas-White-Red River Basins.* National Park Service.

Strong, W.D.
 1935 "An Introduction to Nebraska Archaeology." *Smithsonian Miscellaneous Collections,* vol. 93, no. 10.

 1940 "From History to Prehistory in the Northern Great Plains." In: *Essays in Historical Anthropology of North America.* Smithsonian Miscellaneous Collections, vol. 100, pp. 353-394.

Sunder, John E., Ed.
 1960 *Matt Field on the Santa Fe Trail.* University of Oklahoma Press, Norman.

Swanton, John R.
 1952 "The Indian Tribes of North America." Bureau of American Ethnology, *Bulletin 145,* Washington.

Taylor, William Z.
    1911   "The Last Battle of the pawnee With the Sioux." *Collections of the Nebraska State Historical Society*, vol. XVI, pp. 165-167.

Thomas, Alfred B.
    1929   "Documents Bearing Upon the Northern Frontier of New Mexico, 1817-1819". *The New Mexico Historical Review*, vol. LV, no. 2 Historical Society of New Mexico, Santa Fe.

    1929   "San Carlos on the Arkansas River, 1787." *Colorado Magazine*, vol. VI, May, pp. 79-92.

    1931   "The First Santa Fe Expedition, 1792-1793." *Chronicles of Oklahoma*, vol. 9, pp. 195-208.

    1932   *Forgotten Frontiers: A Study of the Spanish Indian Policy of Don Juan Bautista de Anza, Governor of New Mexico, 1777-87*. University of Oklahoma Press, Norman.

    1935   *After Coronado: Spanish Exploration Northeast of New Mexico, 1696-1727*. University of Oklahoma Press, Norman.

    1940   *The Plains Indians and New Mexico, 1751-1778*. Coronado Historical Series, vol. XI. University of New Mexico Press, Albuquerque.

    1941   *Teodoro de Croix and the Northern Frontier of New Spain, 1776-1783*. University of Oklahoma Press, Norman.

Tiller, Veronica E. Velarde
    1983   *The Jicarilla Apache Tribe, A History, 1846-1970*. University of Nebraska Press, Lincoln.

Trenholm, Virginia C. and Maurine Carley
    1964   *The Shoshonis, Sentinels of the Rockies*. University of Oklahoma Press, Norman.

Trenholm, Virginia
    1970   *The Arapahoes, Our People*. University of Oklahoma Press, Norman.

Twitchell, Ralph E.
    1914   *The Spanish Archives of New Mexico*. 2 vols. Cedar Rapids: The Torch Press.

Tyler, S. Lyman and H. Darrel Taylor
    1958   "The Report of Fray Alonso de Posada in Relation to Quivira and Teguayo." *New Mexico Historical Review*, vol. 33, no. 4, pp. 285-314.

U.S. Army, Corps of Topographical Engineers
    1857   [Exploration from Fort Riley to Bridger's Pass.] House Ex. Doc., 35th Congress, 1st Session, no. 2. pp. 455-520. Washington.

U.S. Bureau of Indian Affairs
    1867   *...Letters of the Secretary of the Interior Communicating...Information Touching on Origin and Progress of Indian Hostilities on the Frontier*. Senate Ex. Doc., 40th Congresss, 1st Session, no. 13. (128 pp.) Washington.

    1880   *Letter from the Secretary of the Interior Transmitting...Correspondence Concerning the Ute Indians of Colorado*. Senate Ex. Doc., 46th Congress, 2nd Session, no. 31, (274 pp.) Washington.

U.S. Department of Agriculture
    1941   *Climate and Man, Yearbook of Agriculture*. Washington, D.C.

Ware, Captain Eugene F.
    1960   *The Indian War of 1864*. University of Nebraska Press, Lincoln. (Originally published in 1911).

Warren, G.K.
    1858   *Exploration in Nebraska; Preliminary Report of Lieut. G.K. Warren, Topographical Engineers, to Captain A.D. Humpherys, Topographical Engineers, In Charge of Office of Explorations and Surveys, War Department*. Washington, D.C. November 24, 1858. In: Report of Secretary of War. 35th Congress, 2nd Session, Senate Ex. Dox., no. 1., Serial 975-976, pp. 620-747.

    1875   *Preliminary Report of Explorations in Nebraska and Dakota, in the Years 1855, '56-'57*. Washington. (Reprint of 1858 report.)

Weber, David J.
    1971   *The Taos Trappers: The Fur Trade in the Far Southwest 1540-1846*. University of Oklahoma Press, Norman.

Wedel, Mildred M.
    1972-1973   "Claude-Charles Dutisne: A Review of His 1719 Journeys." *Great Plains Journal*, vol. 12, pp. 4-25, 146-173.

    1974   "The Bernard de la Harpe Historiography on French Colonial Louisiana." *Louisiana Studies*, vol. XIII, no. 1, pp. 9-67.

    1981   "The Deer Creek Site, Oklahoma: A Wichita Village Sometimes Called Ferdinandina, An Ethnohistorian's View." *Oklahoma Historical Society Series in Anthropology*, 5.

1982   "The Wichita Indians in the Arkansas River Basin." In: *Plains Indian Studies*, D.H. Ubelaker and H.J. Viola, Eds. Smithsonian Contributions to Anthropology, no. 30, pp. 118-134.

Wedel, Waldo R.

1935   "Salina I: A Prehistoric Village Sites in McPherson County, Kansas." *Nebraska History Magazine*, vol. XV, no. 3, pp. 239-250.

1936   "An Introduction to Pawnee Archaeology." Bureau of American Ethnology, *Bulletin 112*. Washington.

1938   "The Direct Historical Approach to Pawnee Archaeology." *Smithsonian Miscellaneous Collections*, vol. 97, no. 7. Washington.

1940   "Culture Sequences in the Central Great Plains." *Smithsonian Miscellaneous Collections*, vol. 100, pp. 291-352. [Reprinted in: *Plains Anthropologist*, vol. 17, no. 57, pp. 291-352. 1972.]

1941   "In Search of Coronado's "Province of Quivira"". *Exploration and Field work of the Smithsonian Institution in 1940*, pp. 71-74.

1956   "Changing Settlement Patterns in the Great Plains." In: *Prehistoric Settlement Patterns in the New World*, G.R. Willey, Ed. Viking Fund Publications in Anthropology, no. 23, pp. 81-92.

1959   "An Introduction to Kansas Archaeology." Bureau of American Ethnology, *Bulletin 174*.

1967   "The Council Circles of Central Kansas: Were They Solstice Registers?" *American Antiquity*, vol. 32, no. 1, pp. 54-63.

1968a   "After Coronado In Quivira." *Kansas Historical Quarterly*, vol. 34, no. 4, pp. 369-385.

1968b   "Some Thoughts on Central Plains-Southern Plains Archaeological Relationships." *Great Plains Journal*, vol. 7, no. 2, pp. 53-62.

1970a   "Some Environmental and Historical Factors of the Great Bend Aspect." In: *Pleistocene and Recent Environments of the Central Great Plains*. Wakefield Dort, and J. Knox Jones, Eds. Department of Geology, University of Kansas. Special Publications 3, pp. 131-140.

1970b   "Coronado's Route to Quivira, 1541." *Plains Anthropologist*, vol. 15, no. 49, pp. 161-168.

1975   "Chain Mail in Plains Archaeology." *Plains Anthropologist*, vol. 20, no. 69, pp. 187-196.

1977   "Native Astronomy and the Plains Caddoans." In: *Native American Astronomy*, Anthony F. Aveni, University of Texas Press, Austin.

1979   "Some Reflections on Plains Caddoan Origins." *Nebraska History*, vol. 60, no. 2, pp. 272-293.

1982   "Further Notes on Puebloan-Central Plains Contacts in Light of Archaeology." In: *Pathways to Plains Prehistory*, D.G. Wyckoff and J.L. Hofman, Eds., Oklahoma Anthropological Society Memoir 3. Norman.

Wedel, Waldo R. and Mildred M. Wedel

1976   "Wichita Archaeology and Ethnohistory." In: *Kansas and the West: Bicentennial Essays in Honor of Nyle H. Miller*. Forrest Blackburn, *et al*, Eds., Kansas State Historical Society.

Wheat, Carl I.

1957   *Mapping the Transmississippi West, 1540-1861*. 5 vols. Institute of Historical Cartography, San Francisco.

Whetmore, Alphonso

1832   *Alphonso Whetmore's Report, In Message from the President of the United States...Concerning the Fur Trade, and Inland Trade to Mexico.* [Senate Doc. - U.S.] 22nd Congress. 1st Session, no. 90, pp. 30-41.

Whipple, A.W.

[1855?]   *Report of Explorations for a Railway Route, Near the Thirty-Fifth Parallel of Latitude from the Mississippi River to the Pacific Ocean.* House Ex. Doc., 33rd Congress, 1st Session, no. 129. Washington.

1865   *Reports of Explorations....* vol. 3. Senate Ex. Doc. 78, 33rd Congress, 2nd Session, Washington, D.C.

Williston, S.W. and H.T. Martin

1900   "Some Pueblo Ruins in Scott County, Kansas." *Kansas Historical Collections*, vol. 6, pp. 124-130.

Wilson, Gilbert L.

1934   "The Hidatsa Earthlodge." American Museum of Natural History, *Anthropological Papers*, vol. 33, pt. 5. New York.

Winship, George P.

1896   "The Coronado Expedition, 1540-1542." Bureau of American Ethnology, *Annual Report*, vol. 14, pp. 329-613.

Witty, T.A. Jr.

1971a   "Archaeology and Early History of the Scott Lake State Park Area." Kansas Anthropological Association *Newsletter*, vol. 16, no. 5, pp. 1-5.

1971b   "Reconstruction of the Scott County Pueblo Ruins." Kansas Anthropological Association *Newsletter*, vol. 16, no. 8, pp. 1-3.

Wood, W. Raymond

1969a   "Two House sites in the Central Plains: An Experiment in Archaeology." *Plains Anthropologist*, vol. 14, no. 44, pt. 2, Memoir 6. Lawrence, Kansas.

1969b   'The Mowry Bluff Site, 25FT35: Architecture.' In: "Two House Sites in the Central Plains: An Experiment in Archaeology." *Plains Anthropologist*, vol. 14, no. 44, W.R. Wood, ed., pp. 6-10, Memoir 6. Lawrence, Kansas.

1961c   "A Contrastive Statement on Upper Republican and Nebraska Ethnographic Reconstructions." In: "Two House Sites in the Central Plains: An Experiment in Archaeology." W.R. Wood, ed., pp. 102-108. *Plains Anthropologist*, Memoir 6. Lawrence, Kansas.

1961d   "Conclusions." In: "Two House Sites in the Central Plains: A Experiment in Archaeology." W.R. Wood, ed., pp. 109-111. *Plains Anthropologist*, Memoir 6. Lawrence, Kansas.

*U.S. Government Printing Office: 1989-674-687/00007